JN125121

Essential Academic Skills
for University Research :
A Historical Studies Perspective

Justin Aukema

大阪公立大学出版会

To my students, past and present.

Table of Contents

Part II: Critical Thinking Skills

Notes on the text:

This textbook is a much adapted and expanded version of a short chapter I published in Kyoto Women's University, Faculty for Contemporary Society, *Kyōjo de manabu gendai shakai*, 2021 and titled "Essential Academic English Skills." In addition, in 2021, I self-published an early draft of this text as *Essential Academic Skills for University Research* which I used in my freshman seminar course that year.

Introduction to the text

1) Aim of this text

A) *Message to students:*

Welcome! This text is for you, first year university students, as you begin your academic journeys at the university. Namely, this text is going to teach you everything you need to know to write an academic research paper for your university courses. Now, you might ask yourself, "why do I need to learn this?" or, "what's so special about writing an academic paper?" Well, because first, conducting academic research is one of the most fundamental skills that you will need at university. Regardless of your major or specialty, you will need to collect data, read texts, handle data, or conduct experiments. And then you will need to compile this information and render it into a coherent format or argument so that you can convey it to other people. This is not easy! And it is way different from simply writing your opinion about an issue, as you may have already learned to do in high school. In fact, while writing is the most important form of academic output necessary to convey information, it is also one of the most difficult things to do. So, do not worry if you have some trouble along the way. Even experienced academics who have been writing and teaching for years still occasionally have difficulty writing and putting their thoughts on paper.

Ok, so what are you going to learn specifically in this text? Well, some of the things include how to choose a research topic, how to organize and analyze sources, how to format your written report, and how to conduct a presentation. Of course, that is not all. Along the way, we will look at many other topics too. These are intended to prepare you for anything that might come your way during your time at the university. By the time you are finished with this course and with this textbook, you will have written your own research paper, made a presentation, and learned *a lot* about a topic that, maybe at this point, you still know very little about. Now, you may go on to research even more about your chosen topic in another one of your university courses. Or you may not. Changing your interests at this point is ok, so there is no need to worry if you decide to give up on your topic later or to keep it. But what really matters is that you are learning the necessary *skills* that you will need and can apply later to any topic that you might eventually choose. All these skills will also help you on your graduation thesis or capstone that you will write mainly in your fourth year of university as well.

One other important message is in order. This textbook traces the research process step by step, from choosing a topic, to completing the final written report. You are welcome and encouraged to follow along with the text as you progress in that your research, too. In other words, you can advance your research and report at the same speed as the text, chapter by chapter. But you do not have to do this. In fact, I recommend getting a head start on your research project and advancing as much as you can at any point. Once you have learned a skill from this text, go out and try it. For example, once you know where to look for sources, do not just spend one week on it, as we do in class. Rather, keep doing it throughout the course. In this way, by the time we reach the end of this text, and the course, you will already be way ahead and have completed a written draft that you can get instructor feedback on.

It should be noted, too, that this textbook teaches you how to write a **research paper**. This seems obvious and self-explanatory, but there are some important characteristics that you need to know about this. First, a research paper has a unique argument 主張 that you make about your topic. We will learn more about how do make an argument in Chapter Eight. But at this point, keep in mind the *type* of paper you will be writing. In this regard, it is similar to what you may have learned of as an "argumentative essay." You may have done this kind of essay in high school, or you may use it on tests such as the International English Language Testing System (IELTS). Second, we are *not* writing a problem-solution essay. This is another common form of essay writing. But it is *totally* different from what we are doing here. In a problem-solution essay, you identify the problem, state why it is a problem, and posit various solutions or strategies to solve the problem. Of course, there are places and times for this type of essay, too. But it is different from a research paper in terms of contents, structure, and overall language and style. You can see more about the differences between these two types in Appendix 1. But, for the time being, keep in mind that research papers have a unique argument that is supported by evidence gleaned during your research process whereas problem-solution essays posit a solution to a posed problem without necessarily being based on empirical source-analysis.

Ok, so that about wraps it up from this end. Good luck as you move forward, and, above all, have fun! The research project is not something daunting or something to be afraid of. Rather, think of yourselves as investigators, private eyes, detectives, investigating sources and trying to get to the bottom of a critical problem facing humanity. It is up to you to identify the problem, gather information, assess the facts, and posit an answer to the question you raised. Learning and critical thinking are an adventure.

B) *Message to teachers (but also useful for students)*

This textbook is designed to teach first year university students the basic steps and strategies of the research project. The flow of the textbook and its contents precisely mirror the research project, beginning with choosing a topic, and closing with formatting the report and conducting a presentation. The textbook is divided into two main sections. The first deals explicitly with the research project. It consists of twelve individual chapters, each one of which teaches a different research skill. The number of these lessons is designed to fit into a single-semester, fifteen-class course with time at the beginning and end for explanation, student presentations, and teacher feedback. In addition, the second section of the textbook deals with other related and ongoing skills that students may find helpful when conducting their research. These last three chapters mainly deal with conceptual topics such as bias in science and understanding the news.

By the end of the course, students will have completed a research paper and a presentation. There is some leeway in how this is taught and the specific requirements that are established. For instance, the length of the report is up to you. However, I typically assign my English as a Foreign Language (EFL) students a word length of about 1,500 English words, or roughly six pages, typed and double spaced. For the presentation, I have students fit within a fifteen-minute time frame, including making time for question and answer. But the text itself is designed for any student regardless of English language ability. Therefore, for native speakers it may be desirable to have a potentially much longer report. In fact, the report structure and model covered here are applicable for a typical journal-length paper or undergraduate capstone paper.

This textbook is written mainly from a humanities perspective and thus does not explicitly address writing and research in the natural sciences. However, many of the skills taught will have some overlap with these other science fields as well. In addition, the textbook gives particular focus to the process of conducting historical research. The biggest reason for this is that my own specialty and training is in History and specifically the history of modern Japan. Therefore, the textbook gives special attention to how to deal with primary and secondary historical sources, how to understand bias in historical sources, and how to analyze historical images. This will be especially useful for students in fields of history, literature, and the social sciences. But, again, using old sources, understanding bias, and tracing the evolution of ideas, for example, are universal skills that transcend any one field. So, in this regard, I hope this text will be an appropriate and useful text for all students regardless of their major.

Relatedly, students are free to choose any topic for their research project in this course. The textbook is written in a general enough way to accommodate for various topics, fields, and perspectives. Of course, I always work closely with each student as they develop their projects, and try to steer them, if necessary, toward more appropriate topics and methods. There *are* limits to the text, after all. For instance, it is not broad enough to cover most natural science experiments done in teams and designed to test new theories or gather new data. But, as for the sciences, this textbook can easily handle the history of scientific ideas, for instance, or even deal with questions relating to the philosophy of science. In addition, other fields including economics will find many of the contents of this text useful and applicable.

C) *Significance of this textbook*

Let's be honest, there are a lot of textbooks teaching research skills out there. So, why do we need one more? Well, for me, the reason for writing this textbook is simple. I just did not find many other textbooks to fit my needs or to accurately meet my satisfaction either. Generally speaking, this mainly relates to my unique teaching situation and background. I have taught at universities in Japan for nearly a decade. The contents of my teaching have alternated between two competing course needs. One was the need to teach EFL students, mainly Japanese, the language skills they would need to complete rigorous collegiate coursework in English. So, in other words, this relates to my practical teaching background, and the real-world needs of my students. But the other need was to teach my field of specialty, which is modern Japanese history. In this regard,

I often found that my students already had some background knowledge in Japanese history (and if I was lucky, even some interest!). On top of this, it was generally easy for me to incorporate authentic, primary historical sources from Japanese history in the original language since students' Japanese language abilities were not an issue. However, learning *historical methods* was a different issue. Many students could read the Japanese language sources, but since they lacked the necessary tools for analysis, they had difficulty interpreting the broader meanings of the texts, not to mention determining their significance when placed in larger historical context.

So, this textbook was born out of these two needs: to address students' English language needs, and to teach them historical methods from the perspective mainly of Japanese history. Now, the first of these I have simply subsumed into the broader academic research process in general. That is to say, this textbook does not make any explicit attempt to teach students English language skills. It is not a language textbook per se, although some teachers may find it useful or applicable in their language courses. Instead, it is designed to teach basic research skills, regardless of language ability. And in this regard, it is targeted for native English speakers and students from around the world. At the same time, some of the source material touched upon is written in Japanese or references Japanese history. Thus, some knowledge of Japanese or Japanese history would be highly beneficial when using this textbook. Similarly, students will find it helpful to have some interest in history and historical methods. This is not a prerequisite or a requirement. But some level of interest would be helpful. Indeed, the ideal target audience for this book would be students of Japanese history and culture who want to learn fundamental historical methods.

This all relates back to my original reason for writing this text and because I did not find the available textbook alternatives very useful for my purposes. From the first category, there are textbooks teaching English language and research skills. But many of these are published by large companies, and, as a result, their contents tend to be very general and not particularly meaningful (in my opinion). I was also disturbed by what I saw as much ideological bias in textbooks published by large companies. This is a very subtle level of bias, but it generally equates to a justification of the status quo of consumerism and capitalism that dominate our present society. For instance, lessons dealing with marketing strategies, finance, and purchasing goods etc. tend to dominate much English language textbook material. Similarly, science or political topics generally tend to be non-controversial such as "how volcanoes operate" or "the structure of English parliament" etc., without engaging in any kind of critical analysis or discourse. From the second category, Japanese history and historical methods, I in fact know very few textbooks that link both of these subjects. There are textbooks teaching students historical methods, true, but not relating particularly to Japanese history. Similarly, there are books teaching the latter, but not the former. There are some excellent textbooks teaching classical Japanese grammar and such, but while their strategy and organization may be similar, their field and aim is quite different. Thus, for these reasons, I have written this textbook as a guide for first-year university students, mainly at Japanese universities. I hope that it can draw on their background and understanding of the Japanese language and history, while at the same time teach them valuable skills of research and historical methods, as well as give them in-context English language learning opportunities.

Thanks for choosing this textbook!

Justin Aukema
Osaka, Japan

Part I
The Research Process

CHAPTER ONE
Choosing a topic

---

1) Choosing a topic

The first step when you begin your research is to choose a topic. In many ways, this is actually the hardest part of the research project. And yet, especially as students, we frequently have to choose a topic at the beginning of class and in a very short time. So, one strategy to deal with this is to choose a topic that you already have some interest in or that you already have some knowledge about. Here are some possible places to look, for starters.

★ A news story that sparked your interest
★ A topic that you previously learned about in another class and want to know more about
★ Something related to your personal experience…something that happened to you or a friend, or which occurred in your community

These are just some of the places we might begin to look when choosing a topic. There are also a few other strategies that we can use to help us. For example, one way that we can easily conduct research that is meaningful to us and to our future readers is to *choose a topic that is close to us*. This means we can start by looking around us, in our own communities and groups. Start small and work your way up, e.g., your town → prefecture → country. Although we might be interested in events happening far away from us, it is generally more difficult to research such topics considering language differences, proximity, and geographical distance. Also, it is generally easier to find and access sources about topics that are close to us.

2) Defining your focus and scope

After you have chosen a topic, you need to make sure that it is neither too broad nor too narrow. In other words, you want to define your focus. Here are some examples of possible student research topics that are both too broad and too narrow.

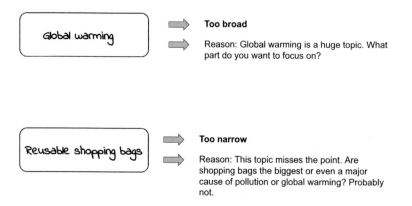

Global warming

→ **Too broad**

→ Reason: Global warming is a huge topic. What part do you want to focus on?

Reusable shopping bags

→ **Too narrow**

→ Reason: This topic misses the point. Are shopping bags the biggest or even a major cause of pollution or global warming? Probably not.

How could we make these topics better? Well, let's think about the first topic. We need to bring the issue closer to us, to make it more personal and more specific. How about something related to energy in Japan? For example, a comparison of Japan's climate goals relating to renewable energy vs. those of another country. Or, even better, local initiatives in your town or prefecture to fight global warming, and a critical evaluation of those.

At the same time, we want to make sure the topic does not get too narrow. Reusable shopping bags is probably too narrow of a topic. First of all, it is too popular and fashionable. Everybody is focusing on shopping bags. But do they really make that much of a difference? Can we solve global warming just with reusable shopping bags? Probably not. This is because they are not really related to the real causes of pollution and climate change. These causes are largely economic and relate to big issues such as class and our current modes of production. So, reusable shopping bags is probably not a good topic either. If we wanted to fix this, we could make it more like the first topic, and focus on various initiatives to fight pollution/climate change in our local communities.

Another important thing to consider is scope. This means choosing a specific date or time-range. If our time-frame is too big, it will be hard to research and write about our topic. For example, "the Edo Period" or "the 20th century" are probably too long of a time frame. Focus on a shorter period of time, for instance "the 1925 Peace Preservation Law" or "the 1980s." I recommend about a ten to twenty year period at a maximum. Anything longer than this will be too difficult to research, because there will be too much source material.

3) Asking questions about your topic

After we have chosen a topic with an appropriate focus and scope, we want to start asking questions about our topic. Below are some common questions we can ask about most topics.

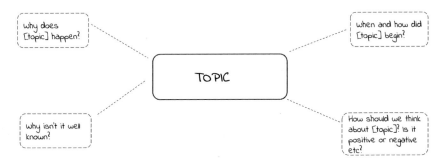

Once we have brainstormed several different questions about our topic, we want to select one question that we feel is especially important and which we want to try to answer in the rest of our report. This one question will become our **research question** 学術問い. It is *very important* that you have a well-defined research question as you begin your research. This is because this question will help guide your research; it will allow you to determine which sources you do or do not want to analyze and focus on.

As you research more about your topic, you will most likely learn more and eventually will find the answer (or multiple answers) to your original research question. Sometimes this answer comes from previous research, and sometimes it comes from our own thinking and data analysis. In either case, the answer to your research question will form your **main argument** 主張 in your research paper.

ASK:

- ❑ Have I chosen a topic that is neither too broad nor too narrow?
- ❑ Have I formulated at least one guiding research question?

CHAPTER TWO
Introduction to historical databases and sources

How do we begin searching for sources? Even though this is just the beginning of your research project, the process may already seem overwhelming. Google, the library, books, magazines, newspapers...so many sources and places to search. Where to begin? In this chapter, we learn how to begin the historical research process.

1) Beginning your search

If you have chosen your topic, then you can begin to look for sources. But where? And what kind of sources? Before you start your search, you need to know the *types* of sources that are available to historians. The two main types are **primary sources** 一次資料 and **secondary sources** 二次資料. In addition, both of these categories include various other types of sources. This is shown in the diagram below.

Primary sources
- Past newspaper, magazine articles, essays
- Diaries, personal accounts, testimonies written by people in the past
- Official documents (e.g. meeting minutes, government laws and proclamations, surveys)
- Old books
- Ephemera (e.g. pamphlets, fliers)
- Popular sources (e.g. children's books, advertisements)
- Images (e.g. paintings, photographs)
- Historical markers, monuments, gravesites

Secondary sources {
- Academic journal articles and studies
- Scholarly books

Of course, this is just a general guideline and not a strict rule. Much of whether a source is primary or secondary depends on how you use it. For instance, if you are critiquing a popular contemporary book or article, this may be a primary source for you. But the general rule is this: if a source is old and from the past then it is probably primary; if it is new or written by a scholar it is probably secondary.

Now that we know the types of sources, we can start our search. You should generally first begin with **secondary sources** and, in particular, scholarly books and articles on the subject. Probably one of the most convenient places to find books and articles is CiNii. CiNii is a database of all university libraries in Japan. From their website, you can search for various types of secondary sources including academic articles, books, and Ph.D. dissertations.

Figure 1: The author's artistic rendition of the CiNii website. You can search for journal or book sources in Japan from here.

But what makes CiNii so convenient is that, even if a book is not in our school's library, you can usually have it sent by mail or have the relevant sections copied and sent to you. In order to do this, you will want to print out or screenshot the page with the information of the source you want and bring it to one of our school librarians. They will instruct you on how to have the source sent to you. One caveat, though, is that to do this you will need to pay the shipping fee for the source.

In addition, you may want to read English language journal articles. One good place to search for these is JSTOR (https://www.jstor.org/). Many universities subscribe to some of the journals here, so you may be able to access some digitally and for free. Other journal articles are available free in digital format. One that I like which deals with Japan and East Asia is the *Asia-Pacific Journal: Japan Focus* (https://apjjf.org/).

TRY:
❏ Using one of the databases introduced above, try searching for a keyword related to your topic. What materials come up in your search results? Do any of these look especially relevant to your topic?

4) Literature review

As a general rule, the first sources you want to gather are secondary sources, i.e., the major academic studies – especially books – on your topic. Most topics that we choose will have at least some books and articles written about them already. If these do not exist, your topic may be either too narrow or unfeasible for our current project. You want to gather these main books and articles and conduct a review of the previous scholarship 先行研究. This will take some time. It is not easy to read long scholarly studies. However, you can make your work easier by sometimes reading just the relevant sections of long books, or by understanding first their main argument, methodology, and some of their examples. When you analyze prior scholarship, there are two things you should do.

A) Compile the data

First, compile the data. You will encounter lots of sources as you conduct your project, and so it is easy to get confused or forget where you read something. So, you need to organize your sources and notes into a database that you make. My advice for this is to use a **bibliographic referencing tool**. Some

of the main ones are EndNote and Zotero. I use Zotero, so this is what I will
introduce here. Zotero looks like this:

Figure 2: A screenshot of Zotero running on the author's computer. Image used
under a fair-use agreement.

You can download Zotero and other bibliographic referencing tools for free.
Sometimes you will need to make an account. There are also paid versions
available. The nice thing about Zotero and others is that you can add sources
directly from database search websites. For instance, if you search from CiNii or
even books on Google and Amazon, by adding a simple browser extension, you
can add the source information directly to your Zotero library.

B) Analyze the sources

Of course, different sources have different characteristics that we need to be
aware of. All sources contain some levels of bias and opinion, for example. We
will discuss these things more in future chapters. What we want to be aware of
here, however, is just the first basic steps. In particular, we want to **take notes** as
we read the source. Some of the things we might include in our notes may be:

Info for notes
- Author's main opinions and arguments
- Important dates, names, examples
- Information that is *particularly relevant to our topics*
- Information that the author leaves out
  - Why do they do so?
- How the source relates to other similar sources on the topic?
  - What is the author's unique angle or argument?
  - How is it different or similar to other sources on the topic?
  - Does it engage with other sources on the topic?
- Main conclusions
  - Any avenues left unexplored?

Another issue is how to physically take notes. Do we write on paper? Or do we type our notes out on the computer. Personally, I like to use both depending on the source and what I am using it for. If it is a book I own and want to read quickly, I might take brief notes on post-it notes or with tabs markers. But if we want to take detailed notes, I recommended the computer and especially the built in tool with bibliographic referencing tools (e.g. Zotero). My detailed notes look like this:

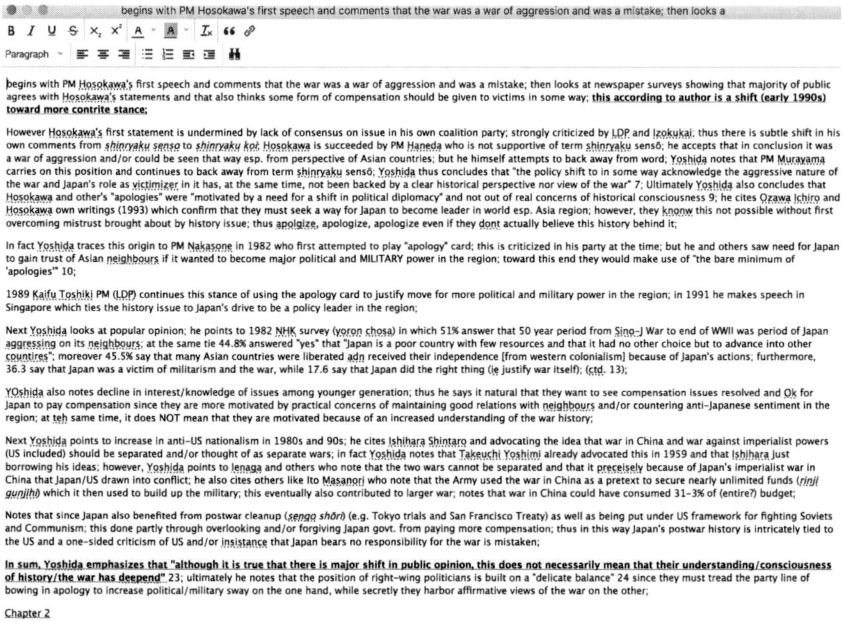

begins with PM Hosokawa's first speech and comments that the war was a war of aggression and was a mistake; then looks at newspaper surveys showing that majority of public agrees with Hosokawa's statements and that also thinks some form of compensation should be given to victims in some way; **this according to author is a shift (early 1990s) toward more contrite stance;**

However Hosokawa's first statement is undermined by lack of consensus on issue in his own coalition party; strongly criticized by LDP and Izokukai; thus there is subtle shift in his own comments from *shinryaku senso* to *shinryaku koi*; Hosokawa is succeeded by PM Haneda who is not supportive of term shinryaku sensō; he accepts that in conclusion it was a war of aggression and/or could be seen that way esp. from perspective of Asian countries; but he himself attempts to back away from word; Yoshida notes that PM Murayama carries on this position and continues to back away from term shinryaku sensō; Yoshida thus concludes that "the policy shift to in some way acknowledge the aggressive nature of the war and Japan's role as victimizer in it has, at the same time, not been backed by a clear historical perspective nor view of the war" 7; Ultimately Yoshida also concludes that Hosokawa and other's "apologies" were "motivated by a need for a shift in political diplomacy" and not out of real concerns of historical consciousness 9; he cites Ozawa Ichiro and Hosokawa own writings (1993) which confirm that they must seek a way for Japan to become leader in world esp. Asia region; however, they know this not possible without first overcoming mistrust brought about by history issue; thus apolgize, apologize, apologize even if they dont actually believe this history behind it;

In fact Yoshida traces this origin to PM Nakasone in 1982 who first attempted to play "apology" card; this is criticized in his party at the time; but he and others saw need for Japan to gain trust of Asian neighbours if it wanted to become major political and MILITARY power in the region; toward this end they would make use of "the bare minimum of 'apologies'" 10;

1989 Kaifu Toshiki PM (LDP) continues this stance of using the apology card to justify move for more political and military power in the region; in 1991 he makes speech in Singapore which ties the history issue to Japan's drive to be a policy leader in the region;

Next Yoshida looks at popular opinion; he points to 1982 NHK survey (yoron chosa) in which 51% answer that 50 year period from Sino-J War to end of WWII was period of Japan aggressing on its neighbours; at the same tie 44.8% answered "yes" that "Japan is a poor country with few resources and that it had no other choice but to advance into other countries"; moreover 45.5% say that many Asian countries were liberated adn received their independence [from western colonialism] because of Japan's actions; furthermore, 36.3 say that Japan was a victim of militarism and the war, while 17.6 say that Japan did the right thing (ie justify war itself); (ctd. 13);

YOshida also notes decline in interest/knowledge of issues among younger generation; thus he says it natural that they want to see compensation issues resolved and Ok for Japan to pay compensation since they are more motivated by practical concerns of maintaining good relations with neighbours and/or countering anti-Japanese sentiment in the region; at teh same time, it does NOT mean that they are increased understanding of the war history;

Next Yoshida points to increase in anti–US nationalism in 1980s and 90s; he cites Ishihara Shintaro and advocating the idea that war in China and war against imperialist powers (US included) should be separated and/or thought of as separate wars; in fact Yoshida notes that Takeuchi Yoshimi already advocated this in 1959 and that Ishihara just borrowing his ideas; however, Yoshida points to Ienaga and others who note that the two wars cannot be separated and that it precesiely because of Japan's imperialist war in China that Japan/US drawn into conflict; he also cites others like Ito Masanori who note that the war in China as a pretext to secure nearly unlimited funds (rinji gunjihi) which it then used to build up the military; this eventually also contributed to larger war; notes that war in China could have consumed 31–3% of (entire?) budget;

Notes that since Japan also benefited from postwar cleanup (sengo shōri) of ties (inkds Tokyo trials and San Francisco Treaty) as well as being put under US framework for fighting Soviets and Communism; this done partly through overlooking and/or forgiving Japan govt. from paying more compensation; thus in this way Japan's postwar history is intricately tied to the US and a one-sided criticism of US and/or insistance that Japan bears no responsibility for the war is mistaken;

In sum, Yoshida analyzes that "although it is true that there is major shift in public opinion, this does not necessarily mean that their understanding/consciousness of history/the war has depend 23; ultimately he notes that the position of right-wing politicians is built on in some way acknowledge a "delicate balance" 24 since they must tread the party line of bowing in apology to increase political/military sway on the one hand, while secretly they harbor affirmative views of the war on the other;

Chapter 2

Figure 3: An image of the Zotero note-taking utility taken from the author's files. Image used under a fair-use agreement.

Once you have gathered the main works of previous scholarship on your topic, you can conduct a literature review. This is basically a short writing ranging from one to tens of pages about what other major works of scholarship there are and what those authors have argued. You might want to summarize each book, for example, in about one paragraph. The reason we do this is to situate our own research and argument within this context. How is our argument different from others which already exist? How are we researching the topic in a way that is different from others? These are the things we need to show at the end of our literature review, after analyzing other works. We will learn more about how to write a literature review in Chapter Five. Along with this, we can also begin to draft a research plan and to make a bibliography. But more on these, too, in later chapters.

4) Continue your search: primary sources

After you have investigated most of the prior secondary scholarship, you should have a good working knowledge of your topic. You may also now know more precisely what you want to argue about your topic and what primary sources you want to look for.

Probably the easiest and best set of primary sources to begin your search with are **newspaper articles**. You can access these from various databases in

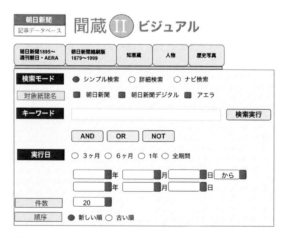

Figure 4: The author's rendition of the *Asahi Shinbun* searchable database.

connection with our school library. Here, I will introduce the *Asashi shinbun* database, Kikuzo II.

As you can see in the image above, Kikuzo II allows you to search for articles by keyword and within a specific date range. Since we are doing modern history here, we can find most of the information we need from newspaper databases like this. Of course, premodern historians will not find this of much use since most newspapers in Japan only date from about the 1870s. Once you complete your search, you will get a list of search results with relevant articles. Your ideal search result number should be at least *below one-hundred results*. If you have more than one-hundred results, your search is probably too broad. You will need to refine either your keywords or your topic more generally.

In addition to the *Asahi*, other major Japanese newspapers such as the *Mainichi* are good places to search, too. Also, you may want to research newspaper articles from around the world. Unfortunately, not all universities have access to foreign historical newspaper databases. The best database to search for this is ProQuest Historical Newspapers. In order to access this, it may be necessary to visit a city, prefectural, or the National Diet library. I will explain more about this shortly.

Newspapers are also not the only kind of primary sources as we have seen. The broad majority of the rest of primary sources are individual magazine and journal articles, old books, pamphlets, and official documents. The best place to find this is at the National Diet Library (NDL). If you can travel to the NDL, that is great. If not, however, you may need not worry. Many of the NDL's sources from before 1945 are digitized and available free online. In either case, you will want to search the NDL website → https://ndlonline.ndl.go.jp

Figure 5: The author's rendition of the NDL online website search tool.

Again, you will get a list of search results after searching. Primary sources take a long time to analyze, much longer than newspapers. So, ideally you want some search results but *not too many*. Probably under fifty would be a good amount to start with. Then, when you actually view these sources, you may narrow it down again to about ten that you will actually want to analyze in detail and use for your research. The NDL also makes some sources available online as mentioned. You can search these sources specifically at Kindai Digital → https://dl.ndl.go.jp/

Other places to find primary sources include city and prefectural libraries. You can search their holdings through their various websites. Finally, here is a list of additional resources and databases that may be useful.

- ❖ 帝国議会会議録検索システム
- ❖ 国会会議録検索システム
- ❖ アジア歴史資料センター
- ❖ 国立古文書館デジタルアーカイブ
- ❖ Lafayette East Asia Image Collection
- ❖ MIT Visualizing Cultures
- ❖ GHQ/SCAP Database Server, Ritsumeikan University

There are other places to search for primary sources, too, which are impossible to cover here. Imagine, for example, that a friend or relative gives you some old photographs, or that you find some old writings at a bookstore. These can be valuable discoveries and ones which are not available in any database! Sometimes it helps to take your search to the streets.

TRY:
❏   Using one of the databases introduced above, try searching for a keyword related to your topic. What materials come up in your search results? Do any of these look especially relevant to your topic?

5) Visiting the library and archives

The next step you will eventually want to take is to visit the library and to use archives. By this point you should have already visited our university library. But there are many sources, most actually, that simply cannot be found in the university library. To obtain these, you will likely need to visit some of the following places:

- ❑ City or prefectural libraries
- ❑ The National Diet Library (either Kansai-kan or Tokyo hon-kan)
- ❑ Historical museums 歴史館・博物館
- ❑ Prefectural or national archives 公文書館

A helpful way to decide which of these to use is to consider *where* your topic is located. So, for instance, if you are researching labor strikes in Osaka you will want to look at historical archives in...you got it, Osaka! Or, if you are looking at the military history of Hiroshima...well, you get the idea. Once you know *where* to look then you can take to Google. Your search might look something like below:

Figure 6: The author's rendition of the Google webpage search tool. Here I am searching for a local history museum in Nagano Prefecture. These can be great places to find sources related to local history, as well as government and other documents.

Once you find the archive you are looking for, do a keyword search on its website to locate specific sources. If you are going to visit the actual archive, you should already know what sources you want *before going*. In the case of many local archives, you will also need to contact archive staff and request permission and a time to see the sources. For the National Diet Library, however, this is not necessary.

Many prefectural libraries do not require you to make a library card. You may simply need to fill out a form and request the materials you want to see. Other restrictions such as copying, taking pictures, etc., may apply. For the National Diet Library, though, you will need to make a library card first *before you can request materials*. Library staff can instruct you on how to do this.

Figure 7: The author's rendition of the NDL library card.

Armed with these new search tools, you should be well prepared to begin gathering materials for your research project. Happy searching! And remember, it helps to share tips and tricks with your classmates. And, to ask the instructor if you get stuck, of course.

CHAPTER THREE
Making a bibliography

So, you have found some promising sources. What is next? Well, after this we want to start compiling a simple bibliography. But, before that, let's perform a simple check to make sure that we are still on track.

Ask:
- ❏ Have I found at least two or three academic books and articles each on my topic?
- ❏ Have I found at least two or three promising primary sources?

If you answered "yes" to the above two questions, you are ready to move on to the next stage. If not, then perhaps you need to continue your search a bit more. Even if you have a topic you like and have formulated a research question, if there are not any sources, it may be impossible to write a research report. Conversely, if you have *too* many sources, this may be a problem, too. It is impossible to analyze hundreds of sources for a class research paper. You need to narrow it down to the *two or three* best academic books and articles, and to have about the same number of primary sources.

SHARE:
- ❏ Explain about one or more of the sources you found to a classmate. What about them appealed to you? How do you think/hope they might be relevant to your topic and project? Conversely, what information might *not* be included in the source(s) you found?

1) Skimming and scanning

Eventually we will start to *analyze* these sources. But you do not have to begin doing that just yet. First, what you really want to be doing is choosing the *best* or *most promising* sources from the bunch. Well, how do we know how to do that? How can we know which are best or better if we have not even read them yet? The key is to **skim and scan**. When we skim, we are just looking at the most basic information such as title, author, and date. Does the title seem relevant? Who is the author? When was it published? This is information we can get from skimming. If a secondary source is *too old*, it might not include the most recent data and information. So, we probably want to stick to more recent secondary sources. We should also skim the table of contents if we are looking at a book. When we scan, we go deeper into the text to search for key phrases and information. We do not "read" the source, per se; we just search for key words and phrases. It may also be helpful to scan any subtitles or headings at this time, too. Why do we do this? Well, it is simple. We want to determine whether the source is really relevant. And, in the case of long sources especially, we may want to skip directly to the relevant *sections*.

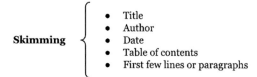

Skimming
- Title
- Author
- Date
- Table of contents
- First few lines or paragraphs

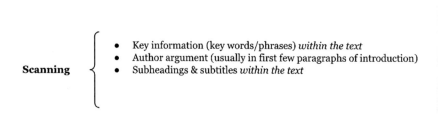

Scanning
- Key information (key words/phrases) *within the text*
- Author argument (usually in first few paragraphs of introduction)
- Subheadings & subtitles *within the text*

Skimming and scanning help us choose just the most important sources that we want to focus on. And it is these sources that we should begin to write in our bibliography.

2) Formatting the bibliography

In this section, we learn how to format a bibliography. But first, what is a bibliography anyway? Simply put, it is a list of all the sources that you used in your research project. More specifically, it is all the sources that we A) obtained information from or B) directly quoted (cited) from. People use different names to refer to a bibliography depending on the aim of their publication and the way in which they use their sources. Some people write "references." This is a list of all the sources, primary and secondary, that were used in the research project but which may or may not have been directly cited from in the final research paper. In a word, it is a list of sources that the author found helpful or useful. Another way to refer to the bibliography is with the term "works cited." This is the most widely used and, for our purposes, the best method. **Works cited** means that the bibliography is a list of all the sources that we directly obtained information or cited from.

Another point to be aware of is that there are different formatting styles when writing in English. This includes Chicago Style, Harvard Style, APA, MLA, etc. Most historians use **Chicago Style**. But which style we choose will depend on the needs and requirements of the course or the publication that we are writing for. We will learn more about the details of different *formatting styles* in a later lesson. For now, what is most important is that *all* the formatting styles include the same basic information in their bibliographies and when citing sources.

Check

How to write a bibliography
There are many different styles and ways to write a bibliography. However, each of them <u>share</u> common features. In general, bibliographies:

A. Are arranged in alphabetical order
B. Include [Author Name], [Article/book title], [Journal Name], [Publisher], [Date], [Page numbers]

In addition to the above points, we may also want to divide our bibliography at first into different *types* of sources that we are working with. Some classes and publications require this, while others do not. But, when we are just getting started with our research project, it may be helpful to do this, just so we can better keep track of the sources that we are using. So, I recommend dividing our sources into our two basic types: *primary* and *secondary*. If we are using a lot of one other single type of source, for example newspapers, we might also want to add a category for that too, e.g. "newspapers."

But, when it comes down to it, the easiest way to explain a bibliography is just to give an example. So, here is one from a recent paper I published below.

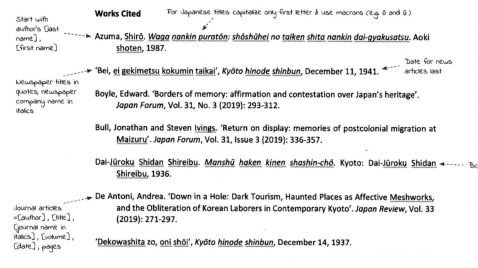

Figure 8: An image of a bibliography that the author previously compiled for a research paper.

Of course, the above example probably will not be enough to answer every question you might have about citing sources in a bibliography. In that case, you will need to consult the format style citation guide directly. Some of the most common referencing styles include:

Common referencing styles:
◆ Chicago Style
◆ The Harvard referencing style
◆ American Psychological Association (APA) style

Note that the online versions of some of these guides are only partial. To access the full guides, you may have to visit the library and check out a style guide book.

TRY:

❑   Using the sources that you have found so far, compile a simple bibliography.

CHAPTER FOUR
Drafting a research proposal

---

1) What is a research proposal?

Ok, so let's review again. Up to this point we have practiced the following things: how to choose a topic, how to formulate a research question, how to find primary and secondary sources, and how to make a bibliography. Now, in this chapter, we are going to move on to the next step: drafting a research proposal. A research proposal is also sometimes called a research plan 研究計画. That means that, in the proposal, we explain what we are going to do and how we are going to do it. Think about it like this. You have a goal. Maybe it is a big goal. Many big goals are hard to achieve suddenly; they take time, patience, and most importantly, a *plan*. So, you write out your goal on paper. Then you write some *concrete steps* you can take to achieve your goal. These things help you focus and decide what you need to do and in what order to achieve your goal. You might also develop a timeline for how long it will take you to achieve each step toward your eventual goal. This is basically the same thing that we do when we write our research proposals.

There is no single way to write a proposal. The type of proposal you write will depend on A) the purpose of the project and B) the type of project you are doing. Common reasons for writing a proposal include the following.

- ❖ For a graduate school program (M.A. or Ph.D.)
- ❖ For a grant 助成金 application
- ❖ Yearly research plans for academics (researchers, professors, etc.)
- ❖ For an undergraduate class project

Let's take a quick look at each of these purposes and their accompanying type of research proposal. First, if you are enrolled in a graduate school program, either as a master's or doctorate program, you will have to write a very detailed research proposal. A typical Ph.D. research proposal, which you would write before beginning writing your dissertation, might be around ten pages long. It could include a detailed explanation of your argument, sources, methodology, case studies, and chapter summaries. Second, grant applications also require you to draft a research plan. A grant application proposal is usually shorter than a graduate research proposal, but it would include the key argument, sources, and methodology you plan to use. Most importantly, it would include detailed explanation of your methodology and case studies. This is because you need to explain *why* you need money and funds to conduct your research. So, for example, if your research requires you to travel abroad to collect sources, you need to explain this in a grant application. Third, most jobs in academia require you to write some kind of yearly research plan. If you are not applying for grant money, they may not need to be so detailed. They could just be a short explanation of your future or current topic, main argument or hypothesis, and methodology. Fourth, many undergraduate classes also require you to write research proposals. Why? Well, because as we have seen, they are essential in academia. But perhaps most importantly, research proposals also help you focus your argument and help you conduct your research. For our purposes, we are only concerned with the fourth type, writing a proposal for an undergraduate course. So, I will introduce this type below.

2) Research proposal basics

Regardless of the purpose or type of your proposal, all proposals generally include some of the following basic elements.

❑   An introduction to your topic (short background info, why it's important and relevant)
❑   One or two of your most important, guiding research questions (you may also include your hypothesis or working argument)
❑   A brief explanation of the main prior research on the topic (and how your research is different)
❑   Discussion of your methodology; also, what main sources or data you will use, as well as where and how you will obtain this
❑   Your timeline (how long will it take you to complete each step and the whole process?)
❑   A short bibliography with your most important primary and secondary sources

Let's consider each of these a bit more. First, you need to briefly introduce your topic. What is it and why is it relevant? So, if you are researching national energy policy, the relevance could be the urgency of addressing global climate change. Or, if you are looking at gender and capitalism, the relevance could certainly be the ongoing descrimination and exploitation of women in society. Next, research proposals usually include one or two of your main research questions. Why is country A not living up to its Paris Agreement goals? Or, why are women still paid less than men for their labor? If you have a hypothesis (i.e., a tentative answer to these questions), you might say something like "...in this paper, I argue that the reason for this is...[your argument]." But, if you do not have an hypothesis or argument yet (don't worry, that's normal!), you might say something like, "...in this paper, I'm going to investigate the reasons behind these issues."

And, in relation to this point, you may also want to address some of the key prior scholarship. By this point, you probably already should have read some major books and articles (secondary scholarship) on your topic. So, you should be aware of those authors' key arguments and approaches, too. Maybe their arguments and approaches will be different than yours. This is a good thing. The purpose of conducting research is to make a *contribution* to existing scholarship: to put forth a new argument, or to present new data and evidence that has not been analyzed before. This will distinguish your work from others'. So, if you have reached this point, in your proposal you could say something like: "Author A argued [argument] and author B said [argument]. However, I am going to show that, in fact, [your argument]."

Also, you should talk about your *methodology*. What is methodology? Well, a simple way to think about it is, what *method* are you going to use in your research. Or, rephrased, *how* are you going to conduct your research? Are you going to rely on personal interviews? Or will you use documentary sources, evidence, and data from a library archive? Will you conduct experiments? These things are all part of methodology. If you are a historian, methodology is usually pretty straightforward. Most historians use *archival evidence* such as old diaries, official documents, and mass media or other popular sources. There are also differences in approach, too. For example, you might distinguish between the *micro* and *macro* level. In other words, will you highlight one or two individual case studies (micro) or look at large datasets over long periods of time (macro). Also, social historians tend to focus on *qualitative* accounts such as individuals' or groups' subjective experiences as recorded in popular sources or diaries, for example. Economic historians, on the other hand, may be concerned with more *quantitative* approaches, and thus look at business' balance sheets, bank loan records, or government fiscal policy. In any case, each of these things relates to the *methodology*: that is, how you are going to conduct your research.

Another important point about methodology is *where* you will find your sources. On this point, you should be fairly specific. For example, let's say you are researching a fairly specific topic: the history of the Kyoto 16th Division Army between the years 1904/5 and 1945. Now, you will not be able to find primary sources on this topic just anywhere. Our school library, for instance, might not have much information or sources on this topic. So, you will need to access specific archives. Especially, the Japan Center for Asian Historical Records アジア歴史資料センター and the Kyoto Institute, Library and Archives 京都府立京都学・歴彩館. You should state this clearly in your research proposal. Moreover, the former (Jacar) is accessible online, so this makes it easy to access. But the latter is *not* accessible online. You need to actually travel to Kyoto and visit the Institute archives. This relates to the next point: your timeline and the feasibility of the project. Taking the example above, maybe we can easily travel to Kyoto. Of course, to do this, we would need to arrange our schedule and confirm the library schedule. It may take about a week. Perhaps we may even need multiple trips, this might take about a month, for instance. But let's say, now, that we want to access archives in Washington D.C. This is much more complicated and would take much more time to plan and travel. We may need a very long timeline of many months even. If we are using grant money as a professional researcher or are a Ph.D. student, this may be acceptable. But for our purposes as undergrad students, it is probably impossible. That is why it is important to confirm our timeline and feasibility of our project early on, and to choose a topic with sources we can easily access. My personal advice is, at this point, to *stick to something local* (i.e. Osaka or Kansai area).

3) Research proposal examples

Next, I will introduce some examples of research proposals that I have done in the past. Of course, not all of them are perfect. But that is ok. Ultimately a research proposal is just a tool to help you focus your aims and ideas.

A) Example one: Master's program course paper

The first example is a research proposal for a graduate study program course that I wrote in 2010.

Tentative Title:
Concepts of Race as Expressed in World War II Propaganda Films

Proposal

This paper will examine concepts of race as expressed through American films made during World War II. Special focus will be given to the Office of War Information's role in the production of propaganda films. The historical backgrounds of Japanese race relations and attitudes toward Japanese before and during the war will also be touched upon.

In addition to the films focused on in numerous other analyses of this subject, this paper will also examine a number of cartoons made during the war period. These cartoons are certainly not alone in their racist portrayal of Japanese when compared alongside other films of the time, however, they are particularly disturbing because of cartoons target audience – children.

Furthermore, possibly because they have only recently been released to the public, little scholarship to this point has focused on the role of these cartoons and their place in American World War II propaganda, as well as the greater climate of racial animosity toward Japanese at the time.

If there is time I will also try to do likewise in my examination of Japanese propaganda film. In other words, examine portrayals of "the other" through Japanese wartime film. The role the War Ministry exercised over the production of films and the measures it took to get film makers to create films of their liking would also be important in this examination.

Bibliography

Daniels, Rodger. *The Politics of Prejudice: The Anti-Japanese Movement in California and the Struggle for Japanese Exclusion.* University of California Press, 1999.

Dick, Bernard F. *The Star Spangled Screen: The American World War II Film.* Kentucky: University of Kentucky Press, 1985.

Dower, John W. *War Without Mercy: Race & Power in the Pacific War.* New York: Pantheon Books, 1986.

Higashi, Sumiko. "Melodrama, Realism, and Race: World War II Newsreels and Propaganda Film" *Cinema Journal,* Vol.37, No.3 (Spring, 1998), pp. 38-61.

Koppes, Clayton R. and Gregory D. Black. *Hollywood Goes to War: How Politics, Profits and Propaganda Shaped World War II Movies.* Berkeley: University of California Press, 1990.

Nornes, Abe Mark and Fukushima Yukio eds. *The Japan / America Film Wars: WWII Propaganda and Its Cultural Contexts.* Harwood Academic Publishers, 1994.

Films

You're A Sap, Mr. Jap. Warner Brothers, 1942.

Know Your Enemy – Japan. Directed by Frank Capra, 1945.

Tokio Jokio. Warner Brothers, 1943

Tokyo Woes. Warner Brothers, 1945.

Victory Through Airpower. Walt Disney

Figure 9: An image of a research proposal for a seminar paper written by the author in 2010.

In this paper I examined mainly American WWII propaganda cartoons (anime). In particular, I looked at how they portrayed the Japanese "enemy" and how these portrayals were predicated on racist stereotypes. The research proposal is a pretty straightforward explanation of what I plan to do in the paper. I also mention the historical significance of the films, namely their powerful impact as tools aimed especially at young audiences. On the second page is my bibliography. This is divided into two sections. The first is prior secondary scholarship on the subject, mainly books and articles which I had found and already begun to read. These were available in my school library. The second section was a list of the films. These were my primary sources. They were all available on Youtube, which made this project very feasible and relatively easy to do.

B) Example two: grant proposal for graduate study program

The second example of a research proposal was written by me in 2015 in order to receive a grant for Ph.D. study.

研究目的及び研究計画

研究目的	本研究では、戦後日本社会において戦争遺跡（戦跡）の記憶がいかに成立してきたのかについて明らかにする。そのため、戦跡を、戦争の記憶が構築される「記憶の場」として捉え、4つのカテゴリーにおいて調査を行う。一つ目は、戦争災害に関する戦跡として広島県の原爆ドームを取り上げる。二つ目は沖縄戦に関する戦跡として沖縄県の旧陸軍病院壕を取り上げる。三つ目は、本土決戦に関する戦跡として長野県の松代大本営跡を取り上げる。四つ目は、軍事施設に関する戦跡として神奈川県の登戸研究所を取り上げる。 それらの調査を通して、本研究は、遺族会や市民団体等 の「記憶のエージェント」が、戦跡において「戦争の記憶」をいかに構築してきたのかについて明らかにする。それによって、戦跡の「保存」をめぐって戦争の記憶が「想起」／「忘却」される「記憶の政治」に注目しながら、戦跡に関する「歴史」と「記憶」の関係について新たな知見を提示する。
研究計画	**平成28年度** 2016年度前半には、長野県において松代大本営跡に関する調査を行う。そのため、関連する文書資料を図書館・文書館・松代大本営平和記念館等において集めるとともに、現地においてフィールドワークを行い、案内板や慰霊碑・石碑等について記録する。また、戦争遺跡保存全国ネットワークの関係者に対して聞き取り調査を行う。2016年6月24–27日には、▉▉▉▉▉▉▉▉ Conferenceにおいて、日本の戦跡に関する研究を発表し、第二次世界大戦の記憶に関する研究を進める研究者らと交流を図る。 2016年度後半には、沖縄県の旧陸軍病院壕跡、及び米国における戦跡の調査を行う。そのため、関連する文書資料を図書館・文書館等において収集するとともに、現地においてフィールドワークを行い、案内板や慰霊碑・石碑等について記録する。また、現地の保存運動関係者に対して聞き取り調査を行う。 **平成29年度** 2017年度前半には、広島県において原爆ドームに関する調査を行う。そのため、関連する文書資料を広島平和記念資料館等において収集するとともに、現地においてフィールドワークを行い、案内板・慰霊碑・石碑等について記録する。また、現地の保存運動関係者に対して聞き取り調査を行う。 2017年度後半には、神奈川県にある登戸研究所の調査を行う。そのため、関連する文書資料を図書館・文書館・明治大学平和教育登戸研究所資料館等において収集するとともに、現地においてフィールドワークを行い、案内板・慰霊碑・石碑等について記録する。また、現地の保存運動関係者に対して聞き取り調査を行う。2017年度後半には、米国における（サイパン、グアム等）戦跡の調査を行い、アメリカと日本側の戦跡にまつわる意識と記憶を明らかにする。当年は、2016年度と2017年度に収集した調査の資料を統合し、本研究の全体のとりまとめを行う。

Figure 10: An image of a research proposal written by the author for a Ph.D. grant application circa 2015.

In the first section, I clearly state the aim of my project as well as my methodology. Namely, my methodology was to conduct fieldwork at four case-study sites. In addition, the second section includes my detailed timeline and steps to complete the whole research project. In my case, the project took two years. Notice that I try to give myself plenty of time to visit each site, conducting fieldwork at two main case studies each year. In addition, I give specific information about what type of sources I will use (archival evidence, historical monuments) as well as the names of the libraries where I can find these sources.

So, as you can see from the above two examples, in order to write our research proposal, we should have already completed the previous steps we talked about. And we should already have begun searching and analyzing some sources, as well as understand where we can access those sources, and have a plan and timeline for gathering them. In my example two, this was a large research project, and so the timeline in the proposal was two years. I received grant money to do this, since I could not pay for travel expenses by myself. But in our case, our research projects will be closer to my example one. It should be feasible to do within the time period of one semester, and we should be able to gather enough secondary and primary sources without having to travel too far away or to spend much money.

Free talk:
- Discuss the progress of your research thus far. You can summarize all of the previous points we've practiced to this point: topic, research question, sources, etc. You might talk about some previous scholarship on the subject. You could also mention where you found sources, or some places that you want to visit (archives, sites, etc.). Alternatively, you might mention some of the challenges and difficulties you've encountered. And of course, questions for the instructor or class are welcome!

CHAPTER FIVE
Conducting a literature review

---

1) Introduction: definition and purpose of a literature review

Ok, so you have found some sources. You have compiled them into a bibliography. You have even thought about your topic and what you want to research. What is next? Well, now you need to *get started* on your project. And the first step to do this is to start reading some of the sources you have collected. My advice is to start with the secondary literature, i.e., the prior scholarship about your topic. If there is a recent book from a major publisher on your topic, this could be a great place to start. Books usually give a broad overview which is exactly what you need in the beginning stages. You want to get as much general information as possible, so that you can increase your own knowledge, and so that you can get a better idea of what precisely interests you about your topic. At the same time, if you are having difficulty finding books about your topic, you might start instead by reading some major journal articles about it. We have already discussed how to find journal articles, so I will skip over that here. But when you read journal articles for a literature review, you should begin with some of the most recent ones and focus on the ones that interest you the most or seem like they would be the most relevant to your paper.

After, or even while you are reading secondary sources related to your topic, you will want to start writing a literature review. What is a literature review? Well, basically it is a summary of the main prior scholarship relating to your topic. There is no set length for a literature review, but for a standard research paper, it might be a few pages long. So, for example, if your total research paper is about twenty-five pages, your literature review might comprise between three to five pages of this. This is just one relative example to give you a general idea of the typical length. The literature review usually comes at the beginning of your research paper, after the introduction.

But wait a minute, why write a literature review in the first place? Well, there are lots of great reasons to do this. But the main reason is to give your reader an idea of where your research fits into the broader picture. So, let's say, for example, that you are researching something related to the history of the Yasukuni Shrine, or the Meiji Constitution. These are big subjects, and there has been *lots* written about them. In other words, yours is not the first study on the subject. And to be honest, it might not even be the best paper on the subject. But that is perfectly fine! Lots of excellent scholars in other words have already done most of the hard work for you. Now, you just need to read their work and briefly summarize it for your audience. This helps you explain the complicated historical background without having to research all of it on your own. So, this is one thing you want to do in a literature review: summarize other authors' previous findings. The other thing you want to do is to summarize other scholars' arguments about the subject. This is important because it will help you establish your argument. You do not want to say the *same* thing about the Yasukuni Shrine, for example, that someone else has already said better, right? No, you want to say something *different* and especially *something new* about it. And the only way you can do this is if you already know what other scholars have written about the subject.

So, to recap, a literature review is a short writing, usually a few pages, at the beginning of your paper in which you explain the contents and arguments of previous scholars' work on the topic.Great. But wait a minute, didn't I just say that literature reviews help us establish where our work fits into the broader picture? How do we do that? So far, we just have a summary of contents and arguments. Well, after you know what other people have already argued, you are now ready to explain how your research is *different and unique*. There are two main ways to do this relative to prior research. First, if a topic or viewpoint has already been previously very thoroughly researched or if there is historical consensus about a certain topic, then there is *less* reason for you to focus on this. There is no need to re-invent the wheel, as the old saying goes. So, one approach, then, is to focus on something that previous scholars have not investigated or have only paid scant attention to. Second, you might encounter an argument in prior scholarship that you *disagree with,* or which seems wrong or mistaken. You could therefore structure your own argument and paper as a counter argument to this and explain why you think your position is the right one.

Once you have done this, established how your research fits into the broader picture, something amazing happens...your own unique argument emerges! We will learn more about how to develop arguments in later chapters. But we have already learned perhaps one of the easiest ways to develop a unique argument about almost any subject. You simply need to read (a lot!) about your topic and understand what all the best experts have already said about it. Once you understand this, you can start to see aspects that have not been researched yet, or which you agree or disagree with. And once that happens, all you need to do is simply to write this down into a simple sentence or group of sentences to form your own argument. But more on that later. For now, let's think more about books vs. journal sources.

2) More about books vs. journals

As mentioned, you want to preferably focus on books in the beginning stages. Books are broad, they are often written for general audiences, and they will give you a lot of information about a general topic. For example, let's say you are interested in learning about Japan's Meiji Constitution of 1889. Of course, this is a big topic. It is too big for a class research paper. So, you need to narrow it down. But, in the beginning stages, you are still not sure exactly what you want to say about the Meiji Constitution, or what aspects of it you want to examine. In such cases, you will want to start with some general and scholarly books on the subject. For broad history topics like this, one great place to start is just with a history book! I recommend the following, for example.

General history book on Japanese history
   ◊   James McClain, *Japan, A Modern History*, W.W. Norton & Company, 2002.

In your search for books on the Meiji Constitution and its drafting, you might also come across some more specific scholarly studies. One great work that deals with the thought processes of Japan's elite leaders who drafted the Meiji Constitution is Carol Gluck's book on the subject. So, this could be another great place to look.

General scholarly studies on the Meiji Constitution
   ◊   Carol Gluck, *Japan's Modern Myths: Ideology in the Late Meiji Period*, Princeton University Press, 1987.

Now, armed with these two books, you are already off to a good start for learning more about Japan's Meiji Constitution. After you have read these two works, you will most likely have a much clearer idea of what precisely you want to research about the Meiji Constitution for your research paper.

So, generally, I recommend starting with books like this. Alternatively, you could also start right away with journal sources. But in this case, there are some things you will want to be aware of. First, journal articles are usually written about much more narrow topics than books. This is partly just due to length: they are shorter than books, so it is not possible to cover as much. Second, journal articles are often focused on making a tightly condensed and original argument. Books, on the other hand, might be less focused on making an argument, and may give multiple, even conflicting views and opinions in order to convey a general overview. So, when using journal articles, you need to be particularly aware of its argumentative nature. This means you should critically evaluate the author's arguments, as well as his or her logical reasoning, and examples, data, and other sources. If all these things check out, journal articles, too, can be great sources of information.

3) What does a literature review look like?

As I mentioned earlier, a literature review is generally a few pages at the beginning of your research report. But what exactly does a literature review look like? How should we write it, and what information should we include? Below, I introduce an example from a conference talk and working paper that I have done on Japan's *gokoku* Shrines. *Gokoku* Shrines emerged from earlier *shōkonsha* which commemorated Meiji loyalists who died in the Bōshin War against the Tokugawa *bakufu*. Later, in the 1930s and 40s, they were renamed as "*gokoku*" shrines, and came to enshrine Japanese soldiers who died in the Asia-Pacific War. They have some similarities, but also some important differences, to Japan's national shrine to the war dead, the Yasukuni Shrine. In my literature review, I started by examining one of the only and most important recent books on the subject, by the scholar Shirakawa Tetsuo.[1] Here is a sample:

---

1) Shirakawa Tetsuo, *"Senbotsusha irei" to kindai Nihon: Jun'nansha to gokoku jinja no seiritsu-shi*, (Bensei shuppan, 2015).

Prior scholarship on G̲o̲k̲o̲k̲u̲ Shrines, Yasukuni, and Japan's war dead

Before presenting my own research, I want to give an overview and analysis of some major works of recent Japanese scholarship on the issues of G̲o̲k̲o̲k̲u̲ Shrines, the Yasukuni Shrine, and Japan's war dead. The most important book on the issue is Shirakawa Tetsuo's 2015 work, *"S̲e̲n̲b̲o̲t̲s̲u̲s̲h̲a̲ i̲r̲e̲i̲" to k̲i̲n̲d̲a̲i̲ Nihon: j̲u̲n̲'̲n̲a̲n̲s̲h̲a̲ to g̲o̲k̲o̲k̲u̲ jinja no s̲e̲i̲r̲i̲t̲s̲u̲-̲s̲h̲i̲* ("Mourning the War Dead" in Modern Japan: Martyrs and the History of the Formation of G̲o̲k̲o̲k̲u̲ Shrine). In the work, Shirakawa is critical of how Yasukuni overshadows issues of the war dead to the extent that the debate simply becomes whether one agrees or disagrees with Yasukuni. He attempts to rectify this by examining G̲o̲k̲o̲k̲u̲ Shrines which, he argues, have different origins and trajectories than Yasukuni. Toward this end, he investigates their origins as s̲h̲o̲k̲o̲n̲s̲h̲a̲ commemorating slain Meiji loyalists, and it is in this context that he makes his main argument. This is that, for approximately the first seventy years of their existence until the late 1930s, s̲h̲o̲k̲o̲n̲s̲h̲a̲ were regarded solely as places to commemorate imperial loyalists from the Meiji restoration and not to enshrine fallen soldiers from Japan's successive wars. Therefore, he says, G̲o̲k̲o̲k̲u̲ Shrines cannot be thought of simply as "mini-Y̲a̲s̲u̲k̲u̲n̲i̲s̲" (68-9).

Figure 11: An image of the literature review section of a work-in-progress paper on Japan's *gokoku* Shrines by the author.

Now, what do I do in this literature review? Well, first, as I mentioned I start with the most important book on the subject. Next, I immediately introduce that author, Shirakawa Tetsuo's, main point and argument in the book. This is that he is critical of how the Yasukuni Shrine overshadows other remembrances of the war dead in Japan. Then, I discuss some of his main historical examples that he uses to support his argument. Namely, Shirakawa shows how *gokoku* Shrines are different from the Yasukuni Shrine, and he highlights their separate histories as *shokonsha* to do this. In the rest of my actual essay, I go into a bit more detail summarizing Shirakawa's book. I also introduce three or four more of the main books written on the broader topic of commemoration of the war dead in Japan. After I do this, I evaluate the prior scholarship. This means that I talk about some of those books' good points and bad points. Then, I talk about what I am going to do in my research paper, and how it is different and similar to what previous scholars have argued. In other words, I re-state my argument which I already stated in the introduction to my paper.

4) Conclusion

In this chapter, we learned how to write a literature review. We saw what a literature review is and why it is important to write one, and we read an example of what one might look like. Now you are ready to start writing yours! As you do so, my advice is to go step-by-step, source-by-source. That means that after you read a book or article on your subject, you can already write up a brief paragraph summarizing the contents and the author's arguments. In this regard, I also recommend sticking with your reading notes. In other words, you can change your reading notes directly into your literature review if you are smart about it and take good notes. Although we do not discuss notetaking in detail in this book, you want to write down the author's main points, examples, and arguments as you read the source. Once you have these things, it is easy to simply turn them into a short paragraph or a few paragraphs of summary. And that summary you can include directly in your research paper as part of your literature review.

TRY: Practice writing a literature review
1) Read one of the sources you've found and take notes on it.
2) In your notes summarize the author's main points, examples, and argument.
3) Rewrite these notes as a coherent paragraph or paragraphs.
4) Practice presenting your one-source review to the class.

CHAPTER SIX
Analyzing historical sources I

---

1) What are historical sources?

In this chapter, we look at how to analyze historical sources. As we saw previously, there are two main types of historical sources: primary and secondary. The first are generally *old* sources from the time period you are studying. The second are *recent* works *about* the time period you are studying (like new books written on the subject). In this first chapter on the subject, we will examine secondary sources in more detail.

2) What are the types of secondary sources and where can I find them?

In previous chapters, we have already seen some of the main types of secondary sources. These are, generally, prior scholarship on the subject, and especially academic books and journal articles. As mentioned, you can search for these on CiNii books or articles. Some are open access, meaning you can view them from anywhere, anytime online. Others, however, you will need to either actually visit one of the libraries that have the sources, or have the sources printed off and mailed to you through inter-library loan for a small shipping fee.

But these are not the only kinds of secondary sources. In this chapter, we will examine more about the types of secondary sources. In particular, we will learn about two main types that will likely be invaluable for your research, and can be excellent places to start and find essential information. These are:

❖ City or prefectural histories 市史、府市、県史
❖ Institutional histories (from businesses, organizations, universities, etc.)

Sometimes these might also be considered primary sources as well depending on how old they are and how you use them. But for our purposes, we are going to assume that these sources will be fairly new and that we will use them to obtain essential data and background information to our topic, as is common with secondary sources.

So where can such sources be found? Well, most city and prefectural histories can be found at, yes, you guessed it, city and prefectural libraries. Unfortunately, most city and prefectural histories are not digitized. But, not to worry, we can still look at the process of how to access and use city histories. And, fortunately, many cities publish information about their histories including tables of contents on their websites. One such example is the *History of Yokohama City*.

3) Example 1: City histories (*The History of Yokohama City*)

Yokohama City publishes information about its city history on its website. I found this via Google search「横浜」「市史」. But you could just as easily find this information searching directly through a city or prefectural library as well.

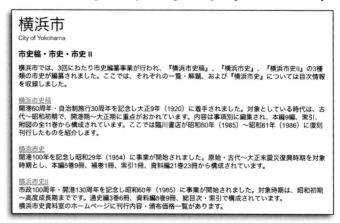

Figure 12: The author's rendition of the Yokohama City webpage containing the City History. Text cited directly from Yokohama City, "Shishikō, shishi, shishiII," October 28, 2020, https://www.city.yokohama.lg.jp/kurashi/kyodo-manabi/library/shiru/history/shishi.html.

As you can see, Yokohama published three city histories, first in 1920, then in 1954, and finally in 1985. Unless we are doing an analysis of how historical representations and consciousness has changed over time, we should access the *most recent* version of the city history since it will have the most up-to-date information. If you click any of the links above, it will direct to you a page where you can find the actual city history books. Again, these are usually always in city and prefectural libraries. But, we can already glean some important information even before actually visiting a library. Take a look at the image below from the same Yokohama website.

巻数	出版年	ページ数	内容
政治編 1	1985	934p	政治編は3巻に分冊し、第1巻は、主として開港前の沿革、並びに徳川時代を通じての民政状態を叙述。
政治編 2	1985	580p, 220p	安政開港より幕末までを叙述。
政治編 3	1985	1002p	明治・大正を叙述。
教育編	1985	1冊	教育の変遷の概況と各学校の位置・沿革を記述。
風俗編	1985	932p, 図版68p	広い意味の風俗方面に関する事相を記述したもの。
地理編	1985	1058, 図版21枚	旧横浜村を中心に次第に拡大された地域の地的沿革を略叙したもの。
産業編	1985	728	徳川時代、明治・大正時代の二期に分けて産業発達の大要を述べたもの。
仏寺編	1986	1002	各仏寺ごとに位置・寺格・沿革・本尊・堂宇・檀信徒数・住職歴代・宝物・史料等に分け記述したもの。

Figure 13: An image of the contents of one of the 1985 *Yokohama City History*. Image is the author's rendition of the Yokohama City webpage. Contents are taken from the Yokohama City webpage: https://www.city.yokoha-ma.lg.jp/kurashi/kyodo-manabi/library/shiru/history/shishi.html.

We can see here what information each volume of the 1985 edition contains. For instance, volumes I, II, and III are about the political history of Yokohama from its time opening as a port city in the Ansei Period (1854-60) through the Meiji (1868-1912) and Taisho Periods (1912-1926). Moreover, we can see that other volumes deal with education, culture, geography, industry, and religion. Therefore, when we access these volumes at the library, we will know exactly where to look. City and prefectural histories are *too long* to read in their entirety of course. We only need specific sections.

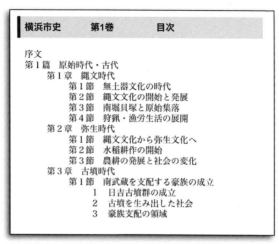

Figure 14: An image (author's rendition) of the table of contents for the 1958 *History of Yokohama City*, available on the city's webpage here https://www.city.yokohama.lg.jp/kurashi/kyodo-manabi/library/shiru/history/shishi1-c.html.

And there is more. As you can see from the image above, Yokohama City also publishes the table of contents of the 1958 version. That version goes back even further in history, all the way to the Jomon Period. So, if we examined Volume I of this version, we could learn about pre-pottery era civilizations, the onset of Jomon civilization, and hunting, fishing, and rice agriculture etc. from that period, too.

TRY:

❑ Look at the table of contents for all of the *History of Yokohama City*. What is some information that we could learn from examining these volumes? Was there any information that caught your attention or looked interesting?

THINK:

❑ How could you use similar city or prefectural histories in your own research? What information might you search for?

4) Example 2: Institutional histories (*One Hundred Years of Keio University*)

The second, very helpful, secondary sources that we can utilize for our research are institutional histories of organizations, groups, businesses, or universities. Most big businesses and organizations eventually put out their own histories. For example, Mitsui has written many books about its origins and company history including the one below, *The History of Mitsui, as seen from Historical Sources* (Yoshikawa kōbunkan, 2015).[2]

Figure 15: An image of *The History of Mitsui, as seen from Historical Sources*. Image rendition by author.

Why are these important? Well, for one, if you are researching, say, commodity histories, for instance, then it is very likely that you will be looking at company histories and trading records. Or, perhaps you want to get business perspectives of major historical events, or to understand the impact that major historical events had on businesses or other organizations. Such institutional histories could be a great source for this information. Yet another reason could be if you are researching the local history of a place. Businesses and universities, for instance, maintain close connections with their surrounding communities. Sometimes so much so that much of the entire population of a given community might be employed by a single company. In this case, the history of that company or organization will be invaluable.

---

2) Mitsui bunko, *Shiryō ga kataru Mitsui no ayumi: Echigoya kara Mitsui zaibatsu*, (Yoshikawa Kōbunkan, 2015).

So, where can you find such institutional histories? Well, if you are researching a large company such as the Mitsui example above, their histories may be published with major publishers and available in bookstores and libraries. If you are investigating smaller organizations, however, in many cases you may have to contact or even visit the organization or a specific library. Some institutional histories are also available online. Let's look at the example of *One Hundred Years of Keio University* published in six volumes between the years 1958 and 1969.[3] These records have been digitized at the National Diet Library, but you need to access them from an affiliated public library. But, luckily for us, some of them are also available on Google books in their entirety and for free.

Figure 16: An image of *One Hundred Years of Keio University*. Author's rendition of the book cover.

- 『慶應義塾大学百年史』上巻
- 『慶應義塾大学百年史』中巻（前）
- 『慶應義塾大学百年史』中巻（後）
- 『慶應義塾大学百年史』下巻
- 『慶應義塾大学百年史』付録

Keio University was one of the first universities in Japan. So, these records offer not only perspectives on the history of the school, but also important insights into the development of the educational system in Japan, one of Japan's most notable liberal thinkers, Fukuzawa Yukichi, and even about modern Japanese history in general. We can get a general glimpse of some of

---

3) Keiō Gijuku (ed.), *Keiō gijuku hyakunen-shi*, Vols. 1-6, (Keiō tsūshin, 1958-1969).

the information in these volumes from the table of contents. From Vol. I, for example:

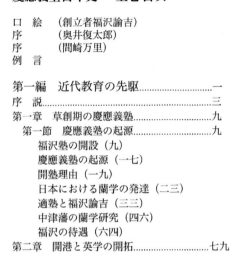

慶應義塾百年史　　上巻目次

口　絵　（創立者福沢諭吉）
序　　　（奥井復太郎）
序　　　（間崎万里）
例　言

第一編　近代教育の先駆............................一
序　説..三
第一章　草創期の慶應義塾...................九
　第一節　慶應義塾の起源...................九
　　　福沢塾の開設（九）
　　　慶應義塾の起源（一七）
　　　開塾理由（一九）
　　　日本における蘭学の発達（二三）
　　　適塾と福沢諭吉（三三）
　　　中津藩の蘭学研究（四六）
　　　福沢の待遇（六四）
　第二章　開港と英学の開拓...............七九

Figure 17: Author's rendition of the table of contents from *One Hundred Years of Keio University*, Vol. I.

Here, we see not only that we could learn about the founding of Keio Gijuku, but also about the introduction of a modern educational system in Japan from the Meiji Period, and about the thought of Fukuzawa Yukichi. Or, again, here is another example, this one from Vol. III (see Figure 18).

If we read some of these sections, we could learn about what it was like for university students in Japan during the Asia-Pacific War (1931-45). And we could learn about the fate of universities like Keio in the immediate postwar, too. So, in other words, institutional histories are important secondary sources because they offer an inside glimpse into how big groups in Japanese society perceived historical events and even the roles they sometimes played in those events.

At the same time, there are certain things we need to be aware of when using institutional histories such as the ones above. For one thing, in many cases, they are not always written by professional historians, but rather by individuals who themselves *are members of* those same institutions. This causes

慶應義塾百年史　中巻　目次

Figure 18: Author's rendition of the table of contents from *One Hundred Years of Keio University*, Vol. III.

multiple additional issues. Professional historians usually cite their sources clearly for others to verify; but non-specialists often do not do this. So, it is sometimes difficult to verify the veracity and accuracy of certain points in institutional histories. More importantly, since institutional histories are usually written by members of those groups, they are frequently biased *in favor of* that organization. For example, the histories above probably are not too critical of either Mitsui or Keio's histories. Certainly, they may undertake some self-reflection and even criticism. But they are prevented by their very nature from writing anything that would incriminate them and undermine their activities in the present. We should beware of these things when using institutional histories. If we can do that, then they can be great sources of information. Incidentally, one way to avoid bias in our own writing when using institutional histories is to clearly identify where the information comes from. For instance, we might write something like: "According to an official Mitsui history…" or "Keio's official school history states that…"

TRY:
❏ Look through some of the volumes of *One Hundred Years of Keio University*. What is some information that we might learn from these sources? Was there anything that seemed interesting or relevant to you?

THINK:
❏ How might you use institutional sources in your own research? Are there any institutions (organizations, groups, businesses) that might have relevant information on your topic?

CHAPTER SEVEN
Analyzing historical sources II

---

1) Introduction

In the last chapter, we looked in detail at the types of various secondary sources and discussed how to use them. In this chapter, we will examine the other main type of sources – primary sources – in more detail. Before that, let's review some of the various different types of primary sources.

Primary sources
- Past newspaper, magazine articles, essays
- Diaries, personal accounts, testimonies written by people in the past
- Official documents (e.g. meeting minutes, government laws and proclamations, surveys)
- Old books
- Ephemera (e.g. pamphlets, fliers)
- Popular sources (e.g. children's' books, advertisements)
- Images (e.g. paintings, photographs)
- Historical markers, monuments, gravesites

One of the key things we can say about all primary historical sources is that they are *old*. More specifically, they are from the actual time period that we are researching. A lot of what distinguishes primary and secondary sources is how we use them. If we are just getting basic information from a source, then we are using it like a secondary source. But if we are actually critically examining a source author's arguments and intents, or the broader significance of a source, then we may likely be using it as a primary source.

This chapter introduces two main types of primary sources: official documents and old newspapers. Let's look at each one of these in order and in more detail.

2) Official documents

A) GHQ documents

From 1945 to 1952, Japan was not a sovereign nation; it was occupied by the Allied occupation forces led by the United States Supreme Commander for the Allied Powers (SCAP) whose office was located in the General Headquarters (GHQ). So, occupation forces are also commonly just referred to as the GHQ or, in Japanese, *shinchugun* 進駐軍, 連合軍, and the period itself is called the occupation period, *senryoki* 占領期 . The GHQ oversaw all aspects of Japanese government from the highest to the lowest levels. In the process, it compiled massive amounts of documents. These documents are now stored in the U.S. National Archives in Washington D.C. as well as at the National Diet Library (NDL) in Tokyo. They are important for what they reveal about Japanese politics, media, and society during the period between 1945 to 1952, as well as about the demilitarization and democratization of Japan.

The flow chart below shows us where and how to find GHQ sources.

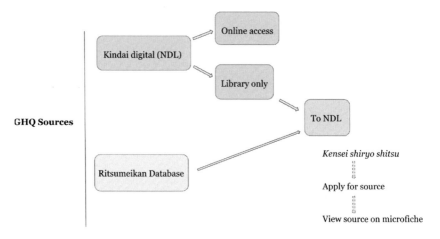

Figure 19: A flow chart demonstrating where to find GHQ sources in Japan and the process to access them.

First, we start by looking in one of either two places: the Kindai Digital archive at the NDL or at a special database server for GHQ/SCAP sources run by Ritsumeikan University. The links for both are provided below.

❏ Ritsumeikan University GHQ/SCAP search tool http://ghq.ritsumei. ac.jp/
❏ General link for the National Diet Library https://dl.ndl.go.jp/

At the Ritsumeikan database, you can search by each individual unit of the GHQ. The main units that will be useful for us are likely CIE and ESS. CIE stands for Civil Information and Education Section while ESS stands for Economic and Scientific Section. In the "Subject" heading for each unit, enter the keyword that you want to search for. Determining the right search keyword can be difficult, since GHQ officials often used different terminology than we do today. Let's say, for example, that you want to learn about the history of Keio University's Hiyoshi Campus. This campus was occupied by GHQ forces for nearly four years during the occupation, since it had also been used as a Navy base by the Imperial Japanese Navy's Combined Fleet during the war. So, in the CIE section, you enter the term "hiyoshi." This yields the following result.

CIE Conference Report (民間情報教育局・会見録)

		Back
Number	43623	
Date	29	
Month	Mar	
Year	48	
Place	Radio Tokyo, Room 604	
Subject	Return of School Buildings at Hiyoshi Campus	
Name	Hiramatsu, M.	
Organization	Keio University	
Division A	Liason Office	
Camera No:	CIE(C)	
Sheet Num Start:	441	
Sheet Num End:	441	

Figure 20: Author's rendition of a screenshot of the Ritsumeikan SCAP/GHQ Database. Showing one search result for the term "hiyoshi."

Of course, this is not the actual source; it is just a *record* of the source. So, you would need to take this information to the NDL Kensei shiryo shitsu and apply for it there. The information you need on the application form is the "Sheet start" and "end" numbers (441).

The other way to find GHQ sources is through the NDL's Kindai Digital website. So, let's try it. Say you want to find information regarding SCAP's policies toward Shinto during the occupation. Because you have read the secondary source literature, you know that SCAP issued a directive called the "Shinto Directive" in December 1945 which banned state support for Shinto shrines and ceremonies (this was important because it affected Yasukuni Shrine). But in all the secondary literature you have read, you have not been able to find the *actual source* of the Shinto Directive. So, you go to the NDL website and search "Shinto Directive." You get 84 hits, probably too many, and so you need to narrow it down. First, arrange the sources by date from oldest to newest. Then, in the left-hand margin, click「日本占領関係資料」to narrow your parameters. Now you have found the source, as shown below.

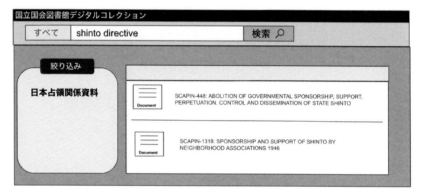

Figure 21: Author's rendition of a screenshot of the search results for "shinto directive" on the National Diet Library's "Kindai Digital" web archive.

What is next? Well, next, of course, we examine the source. If we click the document, we can view it in our browser. There is also an option to save the whole document as a PDF file on our computers. Either one is fine. When we examine primary sources especially we should be certain that we carefully store the source and keep records of it. When I analyze primary sources of a particular category, I often create a separate Word file in which I keep notes as I read the source. Whatever works for you, you should find a place on your computer or hard drive to save the source, and develop a note-taking system for primary sources. Note, you can also utilize Zotero or another bibliographic referencing system here, as I discussed in a previous chapter.

Let's look at the SCAP Shinto Directive in more detail.

1.   In order to free the Japanese people from direct or indirect compulsion
to believe or profess to believe in a religion or cult officially designated
by the state, and

     In order to lift from the Japanese people the burden of cumpulsory
[sic] financial support of an ideology which has contributed to their war
guilt, defeat, suffering, privation, and present deplorable condition, and

     In order to prevent a recurrence of the perversion of Shinto theory and
beliefs into militaristic and ultra-nationalistic propaganda designed to
delude the Japanese people and lead them into wars of aggression, and

     In order to assist the Japanese people in a rededication of their
national life to building a new Japan based upon ideals of perpetual peace
and democracy,

     It is hereby directed that:

     a.   The sponsorship, support, perpetuation, control and dissemination
of Shinto by the Japanese national, prefectural, and local governments, or
by public officials, subordinates, and employees acting in their official
capacity are prohibited and will cease immediately.

Figure 22: Author's rendition of the 1945 "Shinto Directive." SCAP/GHQ, "Shinto Directive," December 15, 1945, National Diet Library, Call No. SCA-1 R2, ID 000006847549.

When we read primary sources, we should constantly be asking ourselves questions. For example: "why does the author say this?"; "what would be the effects of this?"; and "did this actually happen or come to pass?" Moreover, we should also remember that *all* sources *always* have some bias. This is easy to identify. Just remember who is writing the source, what their rank/position is, and then consider how those things might have influenced their worldviews and judgements. You might also want to consider counter perspectives, which you could obtain by analyzing the primary sources of other groups as well. A key way to separate our own views from those of the source author is simply to say "[NAME SOURCE] stated that…" or [NAME AUTHOR] wrote that…" This lets our readers know that it is the source talking and not ourselves, per se.

So, considering the above, let's analyze the Shinto Directive.

1) Why did SCAP say it was issuing the directive?
2) How did SCAP portray State Shinto?
3) What does this say about how SCAP viewed Japan's war responsibility?
4) What specifically was the directive designed to do?

The Shinto Directive is an important historical source. It tells us much about how SCAP viewed Japan's war responsibility and its goals for creating a new Japan in the postwar. If we could answer the above questions, we will already have a good idea not only of the occupation period in Japan, but also about how to analyze primary sources.

B) Japanese Diet meeting minutes

Another great primary source are Japanese national and prefectural diet meeting minutes. In most cases you can search for these online. The national diet records are all searchable and open online. Many prefectural diet meeting minutes, too, are searchable, but in many cases only recent records are viewable online.

To illustrate how such meeting minutes can be used, let me give a story from my own research. I wrote my Ph.D. dissertation on war sites (*senso iseki*) in Japan. One of my case studies was the 32nd Army Headquarter tunnels underneath Shuri Castle in Okinawa. In 2011-12 the Okinawa Prefectural government erected an historical marker explaining the tunnel's history near the site. But, without consulting the committee of historians who wrote the marker text, the governor's office deleted some key passages of the text regarding the presence of "comfort women (*ianfu*)" in the tunnels. I first learned about this history after reading the following news article in the *Ryukyu Shinpo*.

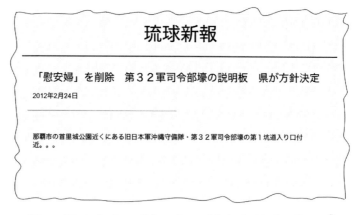

Figure 23: Author's rendition of an article in the *Ryukyu Shinpo*.[4]

---

4) "Ianfu" o sakujo, dai 32 gun shireibu-gō no setsumei-ban, ken ga hōshin kettei, *Ryūkyū Shinpo*, February 24, 2012.

I wanted to learn more about this particular case. Why did the governor's office erase these key passages? What were various Okinawan politicians saying about the issue? In order to find out more about these questions, I decided to investigate the meeting minutes of the Okinawan Prefectural Assembly (沖縄県議会議事録).

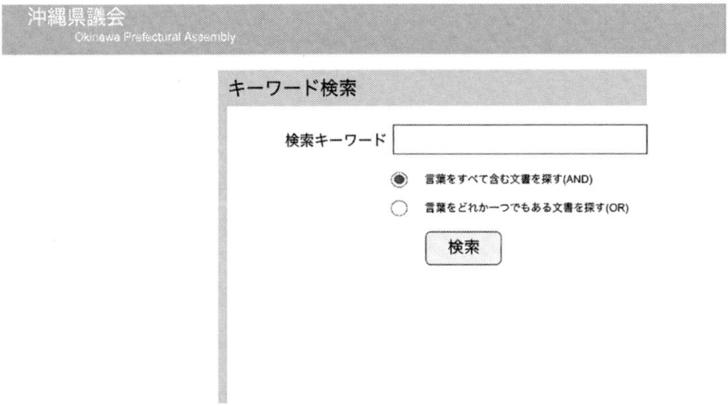

Figure 24: Author's rendition of a screenshot of the Okinawa Prefectural Assembly search tool page.

Fortunately, the Okinawa Prefectural Assembly records are all searchable online (see above image). From this search portal, I entered the key word「第32軍司令部壕」. This was the name of the war site that I was researching. This yielded approximately seventy-seven hits, which is quite a bit. Fortunately, thanks to the above news article, however, I already knew the exact dates, 2011-12, that I wanted to search. So, from the search results, I found entries from these dates. And, sure enough, there was information about the historical marker. For instance, there was the following exchange between Kayo Sogi from the Japan Communist Party and Shimoji Hiroshi from the Environment and Life Division of the governor's office (see Figure 25).

In fact, there were many more debates in the Okinawa Prefectural Assembly about this topic. But from this exchange I already learned that the governor's office approved the deletion of contentious passages about the "comfort women." Moreover, I could glean their stated reasons for doing this. Shimoji said, for instance, that the role of the marker was to explain the loss of Shuri Castle and not the tunnel's whole history. Moreover, Shimoji seemed to deny or question the presence of "comfort women" in the tunnels, despite the fact that there are many first hand testimonies attesting to their presence (see Figure 26).

| 前発言 | 平成24年第一回沖縄県議会
髙陽宗儀 | 第4号2月24日 | 次発言 |

おはようございます。
　日本共産党を代表して質問をいたしますけれども、通告の前にきょうの新聞、タイムス、新報にこういう記事が躍っています。「「慰安婦」「住民虐殺」削る」、「「慰安婦」を削除」というのが第32軍司令部壕の説明板から削除されているという問題であります。これについては、質問通告後明らかになった問題でありますので、議事課にも連絡して先例を踏まえて、この件についてまずは質問をします。
　1、県が策定した「第32軍司令部壕保存・公開基本計画」における基本理念と、説明板設置の目的についてお伺いします。
　2、沖縄戦は、沖縄を捨て石にし、本土決戦、国体護持のための時間稼ぎの戦争ではなかったのか。
　3、今回の「慰安婦」、「住民虐殺」の文言の削除は、知事の指示によるものか。
　4、部長は検討委員会の専門員より沖縄戦について研究しているのか。検討委員会が設置された意味は何か。
　5、さきの戦争を正義の戦争と美化し、日本軍による沖縄の住民虐殺もなかったとする勢力の動きに屈服せず、沖縄戦の歴史の真実、実相を正しく伝えるのが県の責務ではないか。
　6、削除した文言は直ちにもとに戻すべきである。
　以下、質問通告に基づいてまた質問します。

Figure 25: Author's rendition of search results for Okinawa Prefectural Assembly meeting records. Okinawa Prefectural Assembly, General Meeting No. 4, Kayo Sogi, February 24, 2012.

| 前発言 | 平成24年第一回沖縄県議会
環境生活部長（下地寛） | 第4号2月24日 | 次発言 |

　次に、旧第32軍司令部壕説明文についての御質問の中で、第32軍司令部壕保存・公開基本計画における基本理念と説明板設置の目的についてお答えいたします。
　「第32軍司令部壕保存・公開基本計画」における基本理念は、壕の保存・公開に係る背景・意義・基本方針から成っております。説明板の設置目的は、壕を沖縄戦の実相を語る重要な戦跡や平和教育、学習の場として活用することであります。
　同じく旧第32軍司令部壕説明文についての御質問の中で、沖縄戦の意味についてお答えいたします。
　今回の説明板設置に当たっては、限られた説明板のスペースの中で第32軍壕がそこにあったことを示し、壕がつくられた経緯、沖縄戦においてそれが果たした役割、壕の存在により沖縄県のこうむった被害――これは文化財の焼失等でございますけれども――などが記載されていれば十分設置目的を果たそと考えており、沖縄戦全体の意味については検討しておりません。
　次に、文言の削除が知事の指示によるものかについてお答えいたします。
　説明板の説明文につきましては、検討委員会からの報告を受け知事に部の考え方を説明し承諾をいただいた上で、私の決裁で決定したものであります。
　次に、部長の沖縄戦に係る見識と検討委員会が設置された意味についてお答えいたします。
　検討委員会のメンバーは、考古学、沖縄歴史教育研究、美術工芸等それぞれの専門家に就任していただいております。検討委員会は、それぞれの専門家の立場から説明板設置について、設置場所、説明板の形状、説明板に盛り込む内容について参考意見をいただくことを目的に設置いたしました。説明板の設置については、沖縄戦についての専門としてではなく、行政の責任において判断したものであります。
　次に、沖縄戦の実相を伝える県の責務についてお答えいたします。
　検討委員会からの報告のあった文案中、県が削除した部分については、県として確証が持てないため削除したものであります。また、壕の中の慰安婦の存在については、存在を認める証言、存在を否定する証言、両方の証言があり確証が持てない中で説明板に存在を認める記述をする判断ができなかったことであります。県としては、検討委員会の文案を否定したものではありません。
　削除した文言をもとに戻すことについてお答えいたします。
　検討委員会からの報告のあった文案の一部を削除することについては、県として十分検討した結果、さきに説明した理由により決定したものであり、文案をもとに戻すことは考えておりません。
　以上でございます。

Figure 26: Author's rendition of search results for Okinawa Prefectural Assembly meeting records. Okinawa Prefectural Assembly, General Meeting No. 4, Shimoji Hiroshi, February 24, 2012.

In this way, prefectural and national diet meeting minutes can be incredibly useful primary sources. Let's try our own search, this time using the National Diet meeting minutes search portal.

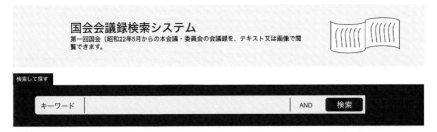

Figure 27: Author's rendition of the National Diet meeting minutes archive search homepage.

> **TRY:**
> ❑ Try searching for a keyword related to your research topic or something else that you are interested in. What kind of search results come up? Is there anything that looks like it may be interesting or helpful? How might you use prefectural or national diet meeting minutes in future research?

3) Newspapers

The next type of primary we will examine is old newspapers. In previous chapters, we learned where to find major news sources such as the *Asahi Shinbun*. Often, by connecting to our school's VPN, we can access the *Asahi* and other newspaper databases even from off campus. When we begin researching any topic, checking the databases of major newspapers is essential. But what happens when we are researching a local topic, or when we want to find out more about local and regional perspectives regarding a specific issue? In these cases, we will very likely need to access the local newspapers of that region, called *chihoshi* 地方紙 in Japanese. Local newspapers allow us to go much deeper into our topics. Unfortunately, most local newspapers are not available or even searchable online. To access old local newspapers, you will most likely need to visit the city or prefectural library of that region, and then view them on microfiche.

Let me give an example from my own research. Previously, I researched the history of the Imperial Japanese Army 16th Division, which had its garrison headquarters in Kyoto. The 16th Division was involved in the Nanking Massacre, so its history is very important for understanding the Second-Sino Japanese War. In particular, I wanted to know how the 16th Division was perceived among Kyoto residents. For example, were popular images of the 16th Division positive or negative? And, how did Kyoto residents' connections to the 16th Division affect the ways in which they understood and remembered the war?

To research these questions, I went to the Kyoto Prefectural Library in Okazaki Park. I knew that the 16th Division was stationed in Kyoto from 1906 until the end of the war. I also knew that the name of the local newspaper at that time was the *Kyōto Hinode Shinbun* (*KHS*). So, I scanned every issue of the *KHS* from 1906 to 1945. This took a very long time – many weeks actually. As I analyzed the news sources, generally I scanned the relevant headlines, then quickly read or scanned any relevant articles while taking notes on my computer. Generally, I was able to get enough information just by reading the news headlines and looking at the pictures.

Figure 28: "Sōkyū ni katsu katsu gunkutsu natsukashi." *Kyōto Hinode Shinbun.* June 6, 1936. Microfiche, Kyoto Prefectural Library archives. Call No. Kyō/k. Used with permission. Image copyright in the Public Domain.

In particular, I was interested in the history of the Nanking Massacre. I knew that this took place mainly from December 1937 and into the following year. So, I paid particularly close attention to those years. Below are some images of articles that I found.

Figure 29: "Nekkyō shimin no geiha e, gaisen ressha tōchaku su," *Kyōto Hinode Shinbun*, June 7, 1936. Microfiche, Kyoto Prefectural Library archives. Call No. Kyō/k. Used with permission. Image copyright in the Public Domain.

Analysis: The first two images, Figures 28 and 29, are both from June 1936 and they portray the return of the Kyoto 16th Division from Manchuria after their deployment there. The division was stationed in Manchuria around Qiqihar and Heihe from April 1934 to June 1936. As these two articles attest, there were very large public gathering and shows of support to welcome the 16th Division troops home from their deployment. This demonstrates the levels of popular support that the division had in its hometown Kyoto. We can also interpret this against the background of Japan's 1931 takeover of Manchuria. Many people in Japan supported these moves and believed the *Kyoto Hinode Shinbun* when it reported that Japan was fighting for "peace in Asia and to maintain the security of Manchukuo" (*KHS*, May 11, 1936).

Analysis: The next three articles, Figures 30-32, are all from December 1937. At this time, the 16th Division was one of the main Divisions attacking the Chinese city of Nanking, the then current capital of the Chinese Nationalist forces. This attack, known as the Siege of Nanking in Japan at the time, later became infamous as the Nanking Massacre in which the 16th Division and other units engaged in the mass murder of Chinese civilians and POWs. How was this attack portrayed in local Japanese newspapers at the time? As we can see from the above, local media such as the *KHS* not only gleefully portrayed the

Figure 30: "Nankin e Nankin e." *Kyōto Hinode Shinbun*. December 2, 1937. Microfiche, Kyoto Prefectural Library archives. Call No. Kyō/k. Used with permission. Image copyright in the Public Domain.

Figure 31: "Nankin otsu! Kyōraku no kofun," *Kyōto Hinode Shinbun*, December 10, 1937. Microfiche, Kyoto Prefectural Library archives. Call No. Kyō/ k. Used with permission. Image copyright in the Public Domain.

battle, but also actively encouraged troops and newspaper readers to support the attack ("Nankin e, Nankin e"). Furthermore, once the city was under the control of Japanese forces, large masses of people in Japan celebrated and held lantern parades, as was observed in the reporting of December 10, for instance. On top of this, newspapers even reported that large numbers of Chinese "enemies" were killed, such as the reporting of December 14 which claimed that 100,000 were killed. It is unclear whether these "enemies" were regular troops in the Chinese military or otherwise. Nevertheless, we can confirm from this reporting that large numbers of Chinese were indeed killed in the Japanese assault on the city.

Figure 32: "Jūman no teki Masani senmetsu," *Kyōto Hinode Shinbun*, December 14, 1937. Microfiche, Kyoto Prefectural Library archives. Call No. Kyō/ k. Used with permission. Image copyright in the Public Domain.

4) Conclusion

This chapter continued our discussion of how to analyze historical sources. Namely, it focused on official documents including GHQ sources and Diet meeting minutes, as well as old newspapers. Toward this end, we learned some places we can go including archives and search tools we can use to find some of these sources. In addition, the chapter highlighted the uses of historical newspapers and discussed some of the ways in which they can be used. In particular, I introduced some old newspapers that I have used in past research. As we saw from these news articles and headlines, old newspapers, especially local ones, can be valuable sources of information. Already from the sources above, we have gained important insights about the history of the Kyoto 16th Division and their reception among and relationship to Kyoto residents. We will learn more about some of the unique characteristics, and pitfalls, of newspaper and media reporting in later chapters. For the time being, let's conclude our practice with the two tasks below.

THINK:

❏   Based on the images of old news sources above, how did the *Kyoto Hinode Shinbun* portray the war and the 16th Division? What can we say about the general image of the 16th Division among average Kyoto residents? What other information can we learn about the war and the 16th Division's roles in the conflict?

TRY:

❏   Use the *Asahi Shinbun* database, Kikuzo II, to search for some sources related to your topic. What keywords did you use? What results did you find? Were there any articles that seemed interesting or particularly relevant to your topic?

CHAPTER EIGHT
Historical sources: image analysis

1) Introduction

In the last chapter, we looked at how to analyze historical sources. Building off that, in this chapter we are going to learn how to analyze and use one type of historical primary source in general: images. Images here means especially photographs, photo-albums, and drawings or paintings. Each of these can be valuable historical sources that can yield information otherwise inaccessible from just print sources. As the common saying goes, a picture says a thousand words. Recently, many historical images have been digitized into easily-accessible online databases. Below, I will introduce some such databases that you, too, can access from home. And, I will explain the various characteristics and uses of each of the three image types mentioned above.

2) Photographs (Database example: public online archives)

One of the most common forms of images especially for modern historians are photographs. Photographs can convey to modern viewers powerful feelings and emotions from the past. At the same time, some photographs may be almost indecipherable for modern viewers. This is especially true of portraits or pictures of past individuals to whom we may have no connection. Such images will need to be placed in their proper historical contexts to make sense. And often this will require extensive work with other documentary sources as well.

Below, I want to give an example from my past research on the historical heritage of Kyoto city that illustrates one way in which images including photographs can be used. In 2017, I read a newspaper article which said that Kyoto's Ponto-chō was going to remove its telephone poles and bury them underground. Advocates of this move said that the telephone poles were an eyesore and that removing them would return Ponto-chō to its more "authentic" historical state. However, I was very curious about the understanding of history in this article. It is true that Kyoto has a nearly 1,200 year long history dating back to the Heian Era. But Ponto-chō was only recognized as a geisha and entertainment district from the *bakumatsu* and Meiji Period. Of course, telephone poles were also introduced into Japan in the Meiji Period. So, it would stand to reason that the "authentic" state of Ponto-chō was actually *with* telephone poles and not without them. But, at first, my idea was only an hypothesis. I needed to verify my claim. And in this case, since I wanted to prove the presence of a physical object, I wanted to look for images rather than just textual sources.

So, the first place I turned was to the Massachusetts Institute of Technology (MIT) Visualizing Cultures database. There, I found an image of a woodblock print produced by Ando Hiroshige III in 1874 which showed telephone poles outside Tokyo's Shimbashi Station.[5] This confirmed what I already knew, that telegraph lines were introduced into Japan from 1869 and were a major part of Japan's modernization process.

This was helpful. But, it still did not tell me anything about Kyoto or about Ponto-cho in particular. To learn more about that, I did a simple web search and located information at the Kyoto City Library of Historical Documents (京都市歴史資料館) about the Fourth National Exhibition for the Encouragement of Industry (*Dai-yon-kai naikoku kangyo hakuran-kai*) which the city hosted in 1895. Over 169,000 of the latest products and technologies from the fields of industry and agriculture were displayed, and over 1.1 million people attended the four-month-long event held in Okazaki Park.[6] In addition, Kyoto Denki Tetsudo Gaisha opened Japan's first electric trolly car that same year in Kyoto. Needless to say, the trolly car, which ran around the main parts of the city, operated with the use of an array of electric cables. From the Kyoto City Library of Historical Documents webpage, I located an image of the Industry Exhibition. Although it did not explicitly show telephone poles, it did indicate the extent to which the city attempted to combine its ancient heritage with the introduction of modern technology.

---

5) Andō Hiroshige III, *Shimbashi Station*, 1874, Accessed at MIT Visualizing Cultures, https://visualizingcultures.mit.edu/throwing_off_asia_01/gallery/pages/Y0185_TOA.htm.

6) Kyoto-shi Rekishi Shiryō-kan, "Kyoto no hakuran-kai," 2008, https://www2.city.kyoto.lg.jp/somu/rekishi/fm/nenpyou/htmlsheet/toshi29.html, Accessed August 19, 2022.

Now I knew I was getting close. Next, I visited the Kyoto Institute, Library and Archive (京都府立京都学・歴彩館) website search engine. I typed the keyword search 「先斗町」 and narrowed my search results to "images." This yielded three results.

京都府立京都学・歴彩館   総合検索 Kyoto Institute, Library and Archives Search

| 先斗町 | x / すべて 🔍 |

1   写真資料
Document   下京第六区婦女職工引立会社仮局

2   写真資料
Document   先斗町歌舞練場 2

3   写真資料
Document   先斗町歌舞練場 1

Figure 33: Author's rendition of the search results for 「先斗町」 on the Kyoto Institute, Library and Archive online search tool.

The second result was an image of the Kaburenjo Theater and dated from the late Meiji to early Taisho Periods. The Kaburenjo Theater was Ponto-chō's most famous attraction, and it was where the Kamogawa-odori and other *geisha* acts were, and still are, performed. When I viewed the larger image file, it was clearly apparent that there were telephone poles in the foreground. I had found the proof I was looking for! (see Figure 34).

What is the point of this example? Well, for one thing, it was simply to introduce various types of databases where you can search for historical images. One was MIT's Visualizing Cultures, the second was online public history sites from official sources, and the third was city or prefectural historical archives' online databases. But another thing I wanted to show through this example was this: images can be used to illuminate things about that past that may have been forgotten, and even to challenge contemporary assumptions about the past. In this case, the contemporary assumption was that telephone poles in Ponto-chō were "unnatural" or "unauthentic." They were not. In fact, the complete *opposite* was true.

Figure 34: The Pontocho Kaburenjo Theater, c.late Meiji to early Taisho. Photo courtesy of the Kyoto Institute, Library and Archives digital archives. "Pontocho kaburenjō 2." Serial No: Shashin 012, Photo No. 466.

Of course, whether or not there were telephone poles in the past is not too groundbreaking and probably will not change the world. But the point is that images can be used to challenge contemporary assumptions. In regards to hotly contested issues, therefore, you can see how historical images could provide powerful evidence to influence thought and behavior in the present.

3) Photo-albums (Example: 第十六師団司令部『満洲派遣記念写真帳』)

The second example I would like to talk about, photo albums, also draws from my previous research. In the past, I examined the history of the Kyoto 16th Division Garrison, a part of the Imperial Japanese Army that was stationed in Kyoto from 1908 to 1945. To learn about the 16th Division's history, I used many old photographs that I accessed from Kyoto City historical archives. Many images showed the 16th Division's activities at the Kyoto Garrison. Of course, armies are not always away fighting wars; rather, most of the time, they are stationed at a home base somewhere. But I also knew that the 16th Division was dispatched to Manchuria twice in 1929 and 1934 before the outbreak of full scale war in 1937. I wondered if I could find any photographic records of their time in Manchuria on these two trips. Fortunately, when I searched the Kyoto Institute, Library and Archives, I discovered that the 16th Division published its own photo album of its activities in Manchuria in 1936.

Figure 35: Author's rendition of the search results for 「十六師団」 on the Three Kyoto Library's Archive online search tool.

The source was titled *Manshū haken kinen shashin-cho* and it was dated 1936.[7] I borrowed the book and began analyzing the photographs. It was a large volume with about three-hundred photos. Each one described the Division's activities around the cities of Qiqihar and Heihe. Each photograph revealed lots of information and evidence. However, it was sometimes difficult to interpret exactly what is depicted in a photo. In these cases, I needed to rely on my background information, to confirm with textual evidence, or to conduct further research to learn the meaning of what was shown in the photos. It is also important to keep in mind the nature of the source. That is to say, who took the photos or compiled them, and who the photos were intended to be viewed by. In this case, the photos were taken by the 16th Division themselves and were intended to be viewed by relatives back home in Kyoto. Moreover, they were clearly intended as *propaganda photos*. This means that they would depict the 16th Division's activities in a way that seemed appealing and heroic. However, even propaganda photos can be important sources for us in the present, because we interpret events differently. Below are some examples followed by explanation.

---

7) Daijūroku Shidan Shireibu (ed.), *Manshū haken kinen shashin-chō*, (Kyoto: Daijūroku Shidan Shireibu, 1936). Kyoto Institute, Library and Archives, Serial Number KO 396.9 D19, Material ID 110296549.

Figure 36: "Autumn [Bandit] Suppression (*Shūki tōbatsu*)," 1934. From Daijūroku Shidan Shireibu (ed.), *Manshū haken kinen shashin-chō*, (Kyoto: Daijūroku Shidan Shireibu, 1936). Kyoto Institute, Library and Archives, Serial Number KO 396.9 D19, Material ID 110296549.

Analysis: This image is important because of the word "*tōbatsu*" ([bandit] suppression). The Japanese military characterized opposition to its occupation of Manchuria as being conducted by "bandits (*hizoku*; see img. below)." However, these "bandits" were not organized military forces but rather included many average people and peasants who had been kicked off their land by the invading Japanese military.

Figure 37: "Captured bandits (*tsukamaeshi hizoku*)." From Daijūroku Shidan Shireibu (ed.), *Manshū haken kinen shashin-chō*, (Kyoto: Daijūroku Shidan Shireibu, 1936). Kyoto Institute, Library and Archives, Serial Number KO 396.9 D19, Material ID 110296549.

Analysis: This image compliments Figure 36. It shows a group of "bandits." Their appearance is more that of peasants than of members of an organized army.

Figure 38: "Burning bandit homes in [unable to determine place name]." From Daijūroku Shidan Shireibu (ed.), *Manshū haken kinen shashin-chō*, (Kyoto: Daijūroku Shidan Shireibu, 1936). Kyoto Institute, Library and Archives, Serial Number KO 396.9 D19, Material ID 110296549.

Figure 39: "Pacification strategies for the Manchurians (*Manshū-jin ni taisuru senbu kōsaku*)." From Daijūroku Shidan Shireibu (ed.), *Manshū haken kinen shashin-chō*, (Kyoto: Daijūroku Shidan Shireibu, 1936). Kyoto Institute, Library and Archives, Serial Number KO 396.9 D19, Material ID 110296549.

Analysis (Figure 38): This image compliments Figures 36 and 37. It shows how the 16th Division dealt with so-called bandits, in this case by burning their homes. This indicates three things: A) that so-called bandits were, in fact, simply Manchurian peasants and not organized fighters; B) that Japanese forces in Manchuria were in fact concerned with capturing and controlling Manchurian *land*; and C) that Japanese forces frequently dealt with so-called bandits in very violent and oppressive ways, including burning their houses and villages.

Analysis (Figure 39): The details of this photograph are unclear. However, it clearly shows a crowd of civilians gathered in front of a stage. It is difficult to see who is standing on the stage, but it seems to be a Manchurian civilian flanked by a person in uniform who may be a Japanese officer. From the caption, we can learn that this is part of Japanese plans to "pacify" the Manchurian people. It is possible that this involved some kind of re-education campaign to emphasize the supposed benefits of Japanese rule.

In fact, there are many more important photographs in this photo album, too many to fully analyze here. Some of them show propaganda fliers that the 16th Division troops distributed to Manchurians to convince them of the benefits and "benevolence" of Japanese rule. Others showed 16th Division soldiers protecting Manchurian railways. Keep in mind that railways including the South Manchurian Railway were a key part of Japanese rule and a way to exploit the material resources of Manchuria. Other images showed memorial ceremonies being held for killed 16th Division troops as well as the ashes of some 16th Division troops being returned to Japan.

What can we say about these images overall? In fact, there is no *single* statement that summarizes all the photographs. Each one tells a very different story. Yet the images do clearly give the impression that the 16th Division's role in Manchuria and the Japanese occupation of Manchuria in general was a period of very difficult, bloody, and violent struggle. This already is quite different from the narrative of Japanese rule in Manchuria as peaceful and benign.

4) Paintings (Database: MIT Visualizing Cultures)

The final category of image sources that we will investigate in this chapter are paintings. Especially, in this case, we will focus on woodblock prints of the Sino-Japanese War (1894-95). Many of these woodblock prints have been digitized and are freely accessible on the MIT Visualizing Cultures Database. The Sino-Japanese War was Japan's first modern war. Japan's Meiji government defeated China's Qing dynasty and extracted huge wartime indemnity (money) as well as gained Taiwan as a colony. It also demonstrated to the world that Japan had become a modern nation, and it shifted the balance of power so that now Japan was the dominant power in Asia.

The Sino-Japanese War was fought before photography was used widely as a technology. This means that in order for people to "see" images of the fighting, they had to rely on older forms of technology such as painting. Woodblock prints were an especially popular way to depict the war. This was an older form of technology popular in Japan from the prior Tokugawa period. Woodblock prints were relatively easy to mass produce, and they were often printed in early newspapers of the time called *kawaraban*. These newspapers and prints were thus intended for mass popular audiences at home, and they had a powerful effect on shaping public opinion of the war.

However, importantly the woodblock print artists *did not actually see the fighting*. Instead, they based their prints on stories that they had heard from wartime news reports. This means that the actual images were entirely imagined by the artists! So, if they are just partly fiction, then why are these important sources? Well, they are important because they show us about popular Japanese images of the war, and about how the Japanese viewed themselves as well as the Chinese "enemy." This means they are also filled with **symbolism** which we, as modern viewers, must interpret in light of the historical background and other evidence. Below are two examples of images.

Analysis (Figure 40): This image shows a Japanese commander, Captain Higuchi, boldly and bravely leading Japanese troops against the retreating Chinese army. Higuchi is shown carrying a young child in his arms. According to a legend of the battle near Weihaiwei, Captain Higuchi rescued a young Chinese child that had been abandoned by his parents. It is unclear whether this story is actually true. However, the symbolic significance of the story and the image is much more important. The symbolic message is that the Japanese (Captain Higuchi) were *rescuing* the Chinese people from the weak and cruel Qing gov-

Figure 40: Mizuno Toshikata, *Captain Higuchi* (*Higuchi Taii*), Meiji Era woodblock print, April 1895. Photograph © 2022 Museum of Fine Arts, Boston, Jean S. and Frederic A. Sharf Collection, 2000.439a-c. Used with permission.

Figure 41: Nakamura Shūkō, *Great Naval Victory off Haiyang Island* (*Kaiyōtō oki nikkan dai-shōri*), Meiji Era woodblock print, October 1984. Photograph © 2022 Museum of Fine Arts, Boston, Jean S. and Frederic A. Sharf Collection 2000.380.11a-c. Used with permission.

ernment. This was meant to convince China and the world that the Japanese were fighting a just and righteous war. Note that the child could also be read as a metaphor for Korea. Japan was ostensibly fighting the Sino-Japanese War to "rescue" Korea from Chinese rule. There are other important symbols in the painting as well. The Japanese forces, for instance, are shown wearing modern military uniforms. This contrasts with the more traditional, "old-fashioned" uniforms and styles of the Chinese. The implication is that Japan was modern while China was still "backward" and undeveloped. Also, the Japanese are advancing bravely while the Chinese are retreating. This implies cowardliness on the part of China. Furthermore, there is much violence in the image, for instance the severed head in the foreground. This demonstrates that violent treatment of the Chinese enemy was not considered a negative thing in Japan at the time, but was rather viewed positively and even heroically.

Analysis (Figure 41): This image shows a Japanese ship destroying a Chinese ship. There is much symbolism in the image. For instance, the Japanese ship is much more advanced and modern than the Chinese ship. This was supposed to give the impression of Japanese modernity and Chinese "backwardness." In fact, although Japan had modernized, many Japanese troops did not have proper uniforms and frequently had to march wearing only *waraji* instead of proper military boots. The reality was that most average Japanese soldiers still had not benefited in any way from Japan's new "modernity." In addition, the Japanese ship is depicted as much larger than the smaller Chinese ship, which is supposed to symbolize military might and strength. Furthermore, the Japanese ship is *white* while the Chinese ship is *black*. This was not an accurate depiction of military ships at the time (battleships are usually not white but are rather black or dark grey). However, the color white is usually associated with *light* and *good* while the color black is often associated, in Western religious imagery, with dark and evil.

5) Conclusion

In this chapter we learned how to analyze and use historical image sources such as photographs and paintings. In sum, images are powerful historical sources that can yield invaluable insights for our research. However, we should be aware of some points when we use image sources. For instance, we should be cognizant about bias: who created the image, what does it *not* show, why does it show some things and not others, and who was it intended for. Many images, moreover, are specifically designed as *propaganda*. All of the images of war above, for example, fall into this category. Old propaganda can, of course, be useful but not in the original way it was intended. Rather, it can show us how people thought in the past.

Many image sources such as the ones above have been digitized and are freely accessible online.

TRY:

❑ Try searching for some images yourself! Use one of the online archive databases to search for historical images. Find one image that interests you and examine it. Consider the following questions:

- What does it depict?
- When is it from?
- Why is it interesting?
- Why might it be a valuable historical source?

DATABASE ARCHIVES:
❑ MIT Visualizing Cultures
❑ Kyoto Institute, Library and Archives Search
❑ 中国戦前絵葉書データベース
❑ Lafayette East Asia Image Collection
❑ 那覇市歴史博物館デジタルミュージアム

*You may also use any other image databases that you find. Many city and prefectural archives and libraries have digital archives with images sources. If you are researching a local topic (e.g. Osaka history) this may be a good place to search, too.

CHAPTER NINE
Crafting an argument

---

1) Introduction

Crafting an original argument is one of the most difficult parts of writing. To make a unique argument, you need to A) know the prior research *very* well, B) have thoroughly conducted your own research, C) have formulated a tentative conclusion or, at the very least, a well-grounded hypothesis. To review the process *prior* to formulating your argument, in other words, you should have already done most of the process below:

Selected a well defined topic
↓
Reviewed major works of secondary literature
↓
Analyzed primary sources
↓
Reached a tentative conclusion (or hypothesis)

After you have done these things, you should be able to formulate an argument. In many cases, arguments emerge naturally. For instance, perhaps you read what most of the secondary literature says about your topic. But when you investigated the primary sources, you found that portions of the secondary literature (i.e., previous arguments) were wrong, partly wrong, or needed revising. Or maybe you also learned new, important information about your topic which had previously not been investigated. If this is the case, then it will be easy to craft an argument because it is clear that what you are saying *has not been said before.*

Note that when I say "argument" here, I am referring to the Japanese word 主張. In English writing, the argument is sometimes also called a "thesis." The argument is also usually only one sentence long, and this sentence is also often referred to as the "thesis statement." But, in any case, each one of these words – argument, thesis, thesis statement – are all translated as 主張 in Japanese.

2) Where do you put an argument?

So, where should you put your argument? Well, put simply, right up front, at the beginning, in the introduction. Specifically, most arguments are stated clearly somewhere near the end of the introduction. But, of course, there are always exceptions. In any case, clearly state in the introduction what you are arguing or trying to show in the paper. It is a common mistake of many even academic writers to forget or to fail to clearly state what they are arguing. This can cause confusion for the reader and can muddle the significance of your entire paper. The argument/thesis statement is *the most important sentence* in your whole paper. It sets the stage for *all* of your later analysis. And, that is why we put it clearly at the beginning of the paper. It is also common to restate the argument/ thesis later, toward the end of the paper, and specifically in the conclusion. But more on this later.

Ok, so the main argument goes in the introduction. But the introduction is just one part of the research paper. What are the other parts? It is important to review this first. The structure of the research paper is as follows.

Structure of the Research Paper

Introduction

(Usually 1~2 paras length)
- ❖ Introduce topic contents (scope, focus, etc.) & historical background
- ❖ Mention previous literature/arguments, research on topic
- ❖ OR...introduce an *unresolved problem* relating to your topic
- ❖ State your argument & why it is novel or how it addresses the unresolved problem that you introduced
  - ➤ Following info, reasons to support or illustrate your arg.; followed by transition to body

---

Body

(Varies from a few paragraphs to many pages in length. This is where you present your main analysis: arguments--reasons--evidence/examples. Note that all of your reasons and examples should support or illustrate your main argument/thesis in the paper.)
- ❖ Discussion previous literature
- ❖ Historical background to topic
- ❖ Results of your analysis & investigation
  - ➤ Relies mainly on your findings from *primary sources*
  - ➤ Is generally limited to 3~4 main examples or pieces of evidence. This evidence could be one or multiple sources, e.g. books, articles, data.
  - ➤ Each reason/examples may be divided into their own paragraphs or subheadings
  - ➤ Generally proceeds chronologically (history papers) from oldest to newest

---

Conclusion

(Varies in length but usually no more than a few paragraphs.)
- ❖ Restate your conclusion
- ❖ Restate the contents of your analysis: scope, focus, reasons, evidence, main findings
- ❖ Concluding sentences, e.g. why your topic is significant, speculation on future development your topic, mention other areas for future research or investigation

---

Figure 42: The Structure of the Research Paper. Composed by Justin Aukema, 2022.

We will discuss the structure of the research paper in detail in future chapters. For the time being, let's just focus on one part of the paper, the part which contains the argument/thesis: the introduction. As you can see, the introduction usually begins by introducing the topic, as well as mentioning the scope and focus. For example, if your topic is historical memories of the Imperial Japanese Army's 16th "Kyoto" Division, and your time period (scope) is A) the period between 1908-1945 and B) most of the postwar, i.e. 1945 to the present, then you might say something like this to introduce your topic:[8]

> *"This paper examines the history of the Imperial Japanese Army's 16th 'Kyoto' Division between 1908 to 1945, as well as historical memories of the 16th Division throughout the postwar period."*

After this, you would probably also briefly discuss the history of your topic (if you are writing a history paper) or give a few more sentences of information about your topic, including why it is important or significant today. Next, you might also mention some of the previous scholarship on your topic, or arguments made about your topic. This is important because, when you craft an *original argument*, you want to show how your research is *different* from previous scholarship. In other words, with your argument, you usually want to answer the question: what does my research do differently than previous scholarship? In addition, another approach would be to present a yet unresolved problem regarding your topic. In the first instance, if we borrow our previous example of the 16th Division history, we might say something like this:

> *"Previous studies have examined the history of the 16th Division in piecemeal, but none have yet provided a comprehensive overview of its history, nor positioned this within the broader history of Kyoto City."*

Or, if we take the second approach, we might say something like this:

> *"The 16th Division acquired a dark and painful legacy after its involvement in the 1937 Battle of Nanking and its near total destruction in the 1944 Battle of Leyte. Yet, in the postwar, the garrison became detached from this history as it was repurposed mainly as a school and two universities. The issue of how to narrate and remember the 16th Division's past is contested at the site today."*

---

8) Each of the examples in this section are from a forthcoming publication by the author. Justin Aukema, "At the Border of Memory and History: Kyoto's Contested War Heritage," In Edward Boyle (ed). *Heritage, Conflicted Sites and Bordered Memories in Asia*, Brill (forthcoming 2022).

Finally, following this, we would state our argument. If we continue on with the previous example, our argument might look something like this:

"This essay argues that the roots of this contestation lie in the underlying tension between history, memory, and heritage."

This argument is, in fact, a bit complicated. But, nevertheless, the important thing to be aware of at this point is A) how to craft an argument, B) where to position an argument, and C) the structure of the introduction. The full example in this case looks like this:

Kyoto usually brings to mind ancient temples or traditional arts and crafts, not war and destruction. But Kyoto's modern history is deeply connected to war. Tangible evidence of this is found in the remains of military facilities from the former Japanese Army and Navy still scattered around the city and prefecture today. This paper focuses on one of Kyoto's most notable military sites, often called 'war sites (*senseki* or *sensō iseki*)' in Japanese: the main garrison for the Army 16th Division which was stationed in Kyoto's Fushimi Ward from 1907 until the end of the Asia-Pacific War. The 16th Division acquired a dark and painful legacy after its involvement in the 1937 Battle of Nanking and its near total destruction in the 1944 Battle of Leyte. Yet, in the postwar, the garrison became detached from this history as it was repurposed mainly as a school and two universities. The issue of how to narrate and remember the 16th Division's past is contested at the site today.

This essay argues that the roots of this contestation lie in the underlying tension between history, memory, and heritage. In the postwar, various memory communities including veterans and war bereaved groups, as well as the garrison's main postwar inheritor, a catholic Women's school called Seibo Jogakuin, laid stake to the garrison, reshaping it to fit their aims and working it into their biographical identities. For these groups, the 16th Division garrison was a 'site of memory (*lieux de mémoire*)', based largely on positive – and highly localized and bordered – interpretations of the past, and which functioned to reaffirm and solidify group identity and narratives of self. Yet as the Asia-Pacific War moved from memory to history, so too did its tangible relics. Later generations of historians and activists from the 1980s sought to clarify the historical significance of the garrison by synthesizing the narratives of multiple memory groups into a critical history of the site. But this undermined previous memory groups' exclusive claims to ownership of the past at the garrison. Moreover, activist-historian's attempts to construct a more cosmopolitan memory by uncovering and confronting painful events from the garrison's past such as the Nanking Massacre, and by including voices of Asian victims of Japanese militarism and the 16th Division in their accounts, drew fierce opposition from the garrison's other stakeholders. The garrison's partial designation as a Cultural Property, Japan's version of cultural heritage, in 2016 seemed to provide no solution to this impasse, either: the 16th Division garrison had become stuck at the border of history and memory. This essay examines how this situation came about, beginning with an overview of the 16th Division garrison's history, continuing through its postwar transformation into a bordered site of memory, and finally concluding with the return of history and the ensuing contestation this has engendered.

Figure 43: A sample of the introduction of a forthcoming publication. Justin Auke-ma, "At the Border of Memory and History: Kyoto's Contested War Heritage," In Edward Boyle (ed). *Heritage, Conflicted Sites and Bordered Memories in Asia*, Brill (forthcoming 2022).

Here is yet another example of an argument situated within a broader introduction. In fact, this passage is an abstract. An abstract comes *before* the introduction and summarizes the topic, main argument, and findings of a research paper briefly in about 250 words. But in many ways it is structured like a condensed version of the introduction, and it contains the argument/thesis statement as well.

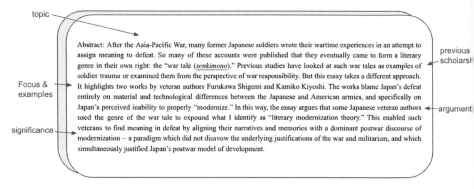

Abstract: After the Asia-Pacific War, many former Japanese soldiers wrote their wartime experiences in an attempt to assign meaning to defeat. So many of these accounts were published that they eventually came to form a literary genre in their own right: the "war tale (*senkimono*)." Previous studies have looked at such war tales as examples of soldier trauma or examined them from the perspective of war responsibility. But this essay takes a different approach. It highlights two works by veteran authors Furukawa Shigemi and Kamiko Kiyoshi. The works blame Japan's defeat entirely on material and technological differences between the Japanese and American armies, and specifically on Japan's perceived inability to properly "modernize." In this way, the essay argues that some Japanese veteran authors used the genre of the war tale to expound what I identify as "literary modernization theory." This enabled such veterans to find meaning in defeat by aligning their narratives and memories with a dominant postwar discourse of modernization – a paradigm which did not disavow the underlying justifications of the war and militarism, and which simultaneously justified Japan's postwar model of development.

Figure 44: An image of the abstract from Justin Aukema, "Modernization Theory & Japanese Veterans' Asia-Pacific 'War Tales,'" *The Asia-Pacific Journal: Japan Focus*, Vol. 20, Iss. 10, No. 5 (May 2022).

3) Key phrases: how to express an argument

Now that we know a little about where to position an argument in our essay, let's examine some of the phrases we can use to actually express our argument. This is not too difficult, and there are usually just a handful of key phrases we can use. In addition to expressing our argument, I will also introduce some phrases we can use for the other parts of the introduction as well, including introducing our topic and discussing previous scholarship.

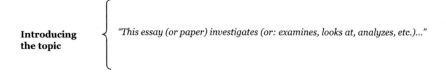

Introducing the topic   *"This essay (or paper) investigates (or: examines, looks at, analyzes, etc.)..."*

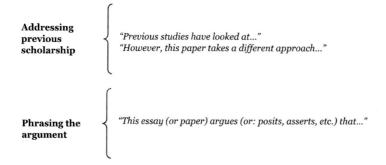

Addressing previous scholarship
{
"Previous studies have looked at..."
"However, this paper takes a different approach..."

Phrasing the argument
{
"This essay (or paper) argues (or: posits, asserts, etc.) that..."

And that is pretty much it. We have now learned A) how to craft an argument, B) where to put an argument in our essay, and C) some phrases we can use to express our argument. Now that we know how to do these things, we can start to craft our own argument. At the same time, before we do this, it might also be helpful to look at some secondary sources related to our topic, especially journal articles, and see if we can identify the authors' arguments. Let's do this as a final exercise and share our results with the class.

TRY:
❑   Look again at the secondary sources you found relating to your topic (especially journal articles). Examine the abstracts and the introductions. Do the authors clearly state their argument at the beginning of their paper? If so, what is it? How do they demonstrate that their argument/research is unique and significant?

CHAPTER TEN
Formatting the report

---

1) Introduction: logical reasoning

Previously, we saw how to craft an argument and where to situate that argument within your report. Specifically, we learned how your argument should come somewhere in the introduction, and typically toward the end of the first paragraph or beginning of the second paragraph of the introduction. This is not a strict rule but more of a general guideline. In addition, in the last chapter, we learned how to format your report more generally. In that chapter, we also examined an outline of the general structure of a research report, including the main parts – introduction, body, and conclusion – and some of the main information that is typically found in each part. This will be an important guideline to follow as you write your own report.

According to the model for the Structure of the Research Report (p.85), research reports (especially history reports, in this case) generally follow certain patterns and include certain information at given points, e.g., a discussion of prior scholarship toward the beginning of the body. But what are the more general and basic parts of a research report? How far can we go toward determining the most *essential building blocks* of a research report?

To answer this question, I suggest that the basis of academic writing is logical reasoning and organization. This sounds difficult, but, in fact, it is quite easy and natural. Simply put, the most common pattern of logical thinking is to state three things in the following order: 1. Argument/statement, 2. Reason, 3. Evidence/ examples. For instance, imagine you are talking about your favorite musician with a friend. You say something like, "I like singer A." Your friend then asks you "why," and so you next explain why, i.e. you give a reason (e.g. "Because she is very talented"). Of course, you might also want to demonstrate *how* talented singer A is, and so you follow this up by saying: "for example, singer A has a beautiful voice and has won many awards." With this simple conversation, you have already used the logical structure introduced above. This logical structure can also be illustrated using what is called the "House Model."[9]

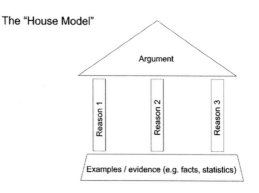

Figure 45: An image of the "House Model" of logical reasoning. Based on a similar model provided by Lubetsky, LeBeau, and Harrington (2000).

In the House Model, the argument or statement comes first; this is like the "roof" of the house. This is supported by reasons or the "pillars" of the house.

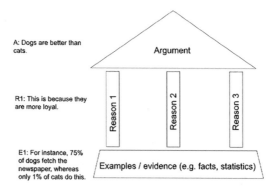

Figure 46: An image of the "House Model" of logical reasoning with examples. Based on a similar model provided by Lubetsky, LeBeau, and Harrington (2000).

---

9) Based on a similar model and example found in Michael Lubetsky, Charles LeBeau, and David Harrington, *Discover Debate: Basic Skills for Supporting and Refuting Opinions*, Language Solutions Incorporated (2000).

After this come the examples and evidence, which serve as the "base" of the house. Each of these three elements (1. Argument = roof, 2. Reasons = pillars, 3. Evidence = base) are necessary to build the house. Figure 46 shows what the house model might look like with another example, this one making a simple argument about pets.

In this example, "dogs are better than cats," is the simple argument. This is followed by a reason (e.g. "because they are more loyal"), which is then supported with evidence, in this case data: "75% of dogs fetch the newspaper." Of course, this is just a silly and simple example. But it is meant to be easy in order to illustrate the key point: that the basis of organizing a research report is logical thinking, and that this process of logical thinking is based on the simple pattern of argument→ reason→ examples given above.

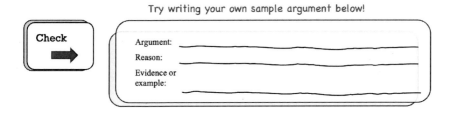

Try writing your own sample argument below!

Check

Argument:

Reason:

Evidence or
example:

2) Logical reasoning & structure

Ok, but how do we apply this logical reasoning and structure to the broader structure of our report? In fact, it is not so difficult to do. I have made a chart in Figure 47 to help us visualize how it would look.

So, what we have here is quite simple: in the introduction we state our main argument. This is the conceptual "roof" of our paper using the house analogy I introduced earlier. Then, in the body of our paper is where we present all of our reasons and examples. Note also that in addition to just reasons and examples, we may have smaller "sub-arguments." Sometimes we cannot fit everything we want to say into one single thesis sentence. And additionally we may want to make further arguments which are related to our main argument but are of slightly and relatively less importance. Keep in mind, also, that every time you make a statement or give a reason which shows why or how something is so, you need to support this with evidence and examples. These things are the meat

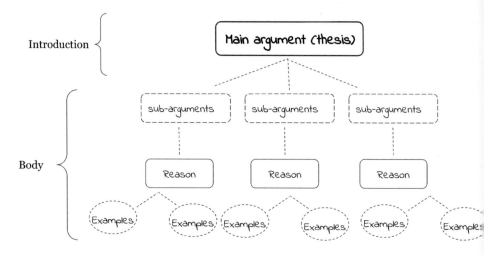

Figure 47: A flow chart example of how to structure logical reasoning within the broader research paper. Composed by Justin Aukema, 2022.

and bones of our research paper; or, to borrow the house model again, they are the pillar and base. Furthermore, notice how every reason and example are all tied to our main argument. Which means that every piece of evidence we introduce in our paper should in some way demonstrate our main argument, or at least the sub-argument we are making in that section. In this way, the use of a logical structure helps to tie our entire paper together.

Of course, the above chart does not list everything that might be given in a research report. For this, you will need to simultaneously consult the more detailed "Structure of the Research Paper" also introduced above. But, it does show you some of the basic fundamentals that are essential to writing a clear, coherent, and persuasive report.

3) Research paper structure example: Kyoto 16th Division

Next, in this section, let's examine some specific examples of how to structure the research paper and how to use reasons, evidence, and examples. The examples I will draw from in this section are from my research publication on the history of the Kyoto 16th Division that we learned about earlier.

A) The introduction

In the introduction, I introduced the background to my topic, its significance, prior research, and my argument. Specifically, I indicate that the history of the 16th Division is only incompletely remembered at its garrison remains and buildings today. I said:

> *"This essay argues that the roots of this contestation lie in the underlying tension between history, memory, and heritage."*

B) The Body

I began the body with some background of the 16th Division. It looks, in part, like this:

A History of the 16th Division Garrison

Part of the reason for the problematic nature of history and memory at the 16th Division garrison has to do with its function as a military base. Military bases are by nature liminal spaces. They are deeply intertwined with their surrounding local communities, often even becoming critical parts of regional economies and identities. Yet for the individual troops who train there, they are transitional places where a short period of months is spent before being deployed. At the same time, military bases become entangled in foreign affairs when troops are dispatched to conduct missions abroad. Military bases therefore interact with the local, national, and global on multiple levels, and they host diverse memory communities (e.g. soldiers and community members) in the process.[4] Concurrently, military bases can become highly contested over the issue of whose memories and histories to emphasize there. Individual memory groups may attempt to write their own histories. But insofar as they fail to account for military bases' multidimensional aspects, they are likely to remain incomplete.

The 16th Division was no different. The Division was stationed in Kyoto's Fukakusa-mura (present-day Fushimi Ward, and a stone's throw away from the famous Fushimi Inari Shrine)

Figure 48: A sample section from a forthcoming publication by the author. Justin Aukema, "At the Border of Memory and History: Kyoto's Contested War Heritage," In Edward Boyle (ed). *Heritage, Conflicted Sites and Bordered Memories in Asia*, Brill (forthcoming 2022).

I began the explanation of the 16th Division's background and history by placing this history in the context of military bases, and I introduced some theoretical discussion about military bases. In the rest of the background, I discussed the 16th Division's move to Fukakusa (Kyoto) in 1908, the establishment of the garrison base there, its size and various functions, and its connections to the surrounding community. I also introduced examples of individual soldiers who were stationed there, and, using their diaries as sources, I showed how they had complex and mixed emotions about the war and the military. Furthermore, I drew heavily on old newspapers from the *Kyoto Hinode Shinbun* to extrapolate the connections between the 16th Division and the surrounding community. Specifically, in this section, I examined how the local newspaper covered the 16th Division's role in the 1937 Nanking Massacre. Why did I discuss this history? Partly to demonstrate an example of my main argument about why the 16th Division history is contested in Kyoto today. The *KHS* beautified the battle and war, whereas individual soldiers frequently wrote about how they regretted participating in atrocities against Chinese civilians. In other words, there were already major differences between various memory groups over how to remember the 16th Division's contested history, even at that time.

After this, I start a new subsection, "The 16th Division Garrison as Memory" (See below).

The 16th Division Garrison as Memory

In the postwar, ownership of former military lands (*gunyōchi*) was transferred to the Ministry of Finance and placed under the administration of various regional finance bureaus. In addition, many former military lands were requisitioned by the occupying Allied forces and maintained their function as military bases into the postwar. Indeed, Kyoto's 16th Division garrison was briefly utilized by occupying U.S. troops and repurposed as Camp Fischer. However, even during that short interlude, the Japanese central government, as well as Kyoto prefecture and Kyoto city were already planning for the site's new postwar applications. This was first achieved in 1949 when it was decided that the site would be the new home of Seibo Jogakuin, a private Catholic women's school (see Figure 10.2).[8]

Figure 49: A sample section from a forthcoming publication by the author. Justin Aukema, "At the Border of Memory and History: Kyoto's Contested War Heritage," In Edward Boyle (ed). *Heritage, Conflicted Sites and Bordered Memories in Asia*, Brill (forthcoming 2022).

In this section, I discussed the postwar fate of former 16th Division Garrison buildings, and examined how the 16th Division was remembered by various memory groups, including former military veterans, bereaved family members, and the new owners of the garrison buildings, namely Seibo Jogakuin and Ryukoku University. Why did I introduce these various groups? Well, the reason, again, relates to my main argument about the 16th Division being contested in history and memory. After the war, various memory groups remembered the 16th

Division in different ways. Veterans had both positive and negative memories; so, too, did bereaved family members; and Seibo Jogakuin officials, too, tended to either beautify or to forget their school's earlier history as a military base. This meant that there was never one single narrative or set of memories for how to remember the 16th Division: rather, there were multiple, conflicting remembrances.

Yet despite the painful nuances of objects and sites associated with the former 16th Division garrison, some veterans and bereaved family member groups found an alternative method of *in situ* remembrance more acceptable: building commemorative monuments. For instance, in 1968 – the same year as the Meiji centennial anniversary – veterans and bereaved family members constructed a two- to three-meter-tall commemorative Monument to the Kyoto Artillery Regiment (Kyōto hohei rentai ato) in one corner of the Fujinomori Shrine on the former 16th Division garrison grounds. In its accompanying description, the monument proudly recounted the 'regiment's magnificent history.' Moreover, it described the 16th Division garrison in the following way:

> The curtain of the past is now attempting to close on and to erase the former remnants of those nostalgic soldiers' barracks of old. Yet the glorious history of our troops, who out of love and concern for their fatherland went forth into battle and offered their lives to the state in its time of need, as well as their honourable traditions, must be forever conveyed to future generations. [...] We consecrate this land as an historical site (*shiseki*) to forever honour and commemorate the meritorious deeds of our brothers in arms who went before us. And we have erected this marker upon this sacred site (*seichi*) of remembrance to bring solace to the spirits of the many heroic war dead (*eirei*), and to offer a prayer for world peace and the prosperity of the nation (On site monument, recorded by the author, February 28, 2020).

Figure 50: A sample section from a forthcoming publication by the author. Justin Aukema, "At the Border of Memory and History: Kyoto's Contested War Heritage," In Edward Boyle (ed). *Heritage, Conflicted Sites and Bordered Memories in Asia*, Brill (forthcoming 2022).

Of course, to support my argument and narrative, I introduced many pieces of evidence. The above is one such example of how I used such evidence. To show how some veteran groups remembered the 16th Division in the postwar, I introduced the example of a 1968 commemorative monument built by a veteran group. I translated the text of the monument, which is cited above: as you can see, the text greatly beautifies and nostalgically remembers the 16th Division.

But, there were also very different examples of remembrances too. The most different form of remembrance came from former 16th Division soldiers themselves. Many former soldiers, especially who fought early in the war, were *very* critical of the war and the military. And in some cases they even wrote in detail about atrocities against Chinese civilians that they had participated in. This viewpoint was so different from earlier remembrances that I dedicated a whole new section to it, "The 16ᵗʰ Division Garrison as History" (See below).

The 16ᵗʰ Division Garrison as History

One important memory group that has so far been missing from this analysis is 16ᵗʰ Division soldiers themselves. Of course, this group was not silent at this time. As historian Yoshida Yutaka has shown, 'war-experience writings' and 'war tales' written by former military men were in fact quite popular during the 1950s and 60s (Yoshida 2005). Some of these, especially those written by lower-ranking soldiers, were critical of the Japanese military, while others written by former officers often beautified or sought to justify the war. What they shared in common, however, was their bordered focus on the Japanese wartime experience and their audience: the wartime generation in Japan. But this changed in the 1970s and 1980s. The Vietnam War prompted some Japanese to reconsider their role as victimizer in Asia during the Asia-Pacific War. The normalization of diplomatic relations with Korea in 1965 and China in 1972, and the return of Okinawa to Japan in 1971 also occasioned reflection on the negative effects of Japanese militarism. In this milieu, some soldiers' wartime accounts became more revealing and critical of Japan's war crimes. And their audiences changed, too. Japanese war memory, by this point, had become an issue of international attention. On top of this, the postwar generation now outnumbered the wartime generation. Lacking the war as common referent for remembrance, postwar generations needed accompanying historical explanation to fully comprehend not just first-hand accounts, but wartime heritage objects as well. In other words, this marked the

---

Figure 51: A sample section from a forthcoming publication by the author. Justin Aukema, "At the Border of Memory and History: Kyoto's Contested War Heritage," In Edward Boyle (ed). *Heritage, Conflicted Sites and Bordered Memories in Asia*, Brill (forthcoming 2022).

Also in this section, I argued that with the passage of time, the 16ᵗʰ Division gradually passed from living memory to history. This means that as the wartime generation aged, there were fewer people alive who had actual living memories of the 16ᵗʰ Division. More and more of the younger generations had to learn about this history from history books. But, this created new problems and controversies. In particular, right-wing historical revisionists emerged who loudly denied that the Nanking Massacre ever happened. Since the historical evidence was not on their side, they instead resorted to intimidation tactics to try to censor history textbooks or to have history museum displays canceled.

C) Conclusion

In the conclusion, I restated my argument that the position of the 16th Division garrison buildings today is ambiguous because the history of the 16th Division remains contested. I positioned this as a conflict between heritage, memory, and history. Here is a section from the conclusion below.

Conclusion
This chapter analyses the contestation over the site of Kyoto's Army 16th Division garrison as resulting from the inherent tension between history and memory. In the postwar, various memory groups such as veterans, war bereaved, and the garrison's inheritors including Seibo Jogakuin, laid claim to the site. For them, the garrison was a 'site of memory' which reinforced contemporary group identity through a particular interpretation of the past held in common by its members. Some veterans and war bereaved saw the garrison as a place to remember and memorialize 16th Division soldiers' heroic sacrifices to the nation. Others at Seibo Jogakuin took a more utilitarian approach, seeing the garrison rather as a means to achieve the school's objectives. Added to this, memories of much of the Kyoto public were largely influenced by wartime reporting which sensationalized and beautified the actions of the 16th Division. These memories were selective and exclusive, focusing only on the parts of the past which suited group members' contemporary needs.[12] They were also bordered and contained, having significance mainly just for involved group members.

Figure 52: A sample section from a forthcoming publication by the author. Justin Aukema, "At the Border of Memory and History: Kyoto's Contested War Heritage," In Edward Boyle (ed). *Heritage, Conflicted Sites and Bordered Memories in Asia*, Brill (forthcoming 2022).

In any case, you can see through this example of my past research some of the points I have tried to introduce in this lesson about how to structure the essay. I introduced examples of how to position the argument in the introduction, how to structure the body including giving a chronological overview of the historical background, and how to use reasons (sub-headings, topic sentences etc.) and evidence to support the overall argument. Now, I hope, you feel a bit more prepared to begin writing your own research essay.

4) Formatting the essay

There is one more point that needs discussing: how to physically format your report on the paper, such as with the proper use of font size and spacing. In general, the most basic format should look something like the example below.

include the following elements.|

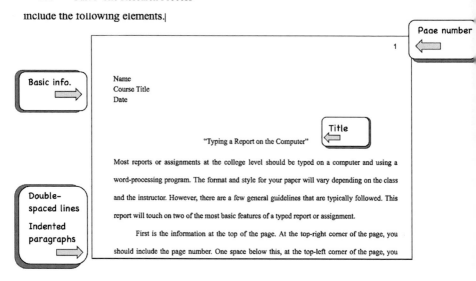

Figure 53: An image of the first page of a research paper and which shows the basic details for how to format your paper. Composed by Justin Aukema.

As you can see in this simple example, the most basic elements you want to have in your report are, first and foremost, your name, the course title, and the date. These should be listed at the top left of your paper. You can also insert page numbers in your report. The above example shows the page number at the top-right of the page. However, I also like to put page numbers centered and at the bottom of the page. Your report also needs a title. This should be centered and approximately four spaces after the date. After that, you can begin the typed introduction. You do not need to indent the first paragraph of each section. But you should indent each successive paragraph. And you should make sure that the whole report is double-spaced and written, usually, in a common font such as Times New Roman, 12-point font.

Of course, there are many other things to be aware of when you format your research report. For example, we have not yet discussed how to cite sources in your report. But, let's save this for our next discussion.

CHAPTER ELEVEN
Citing sources

---

1) Introduction

When we write a research paper, we use lots of sources. This includes the use of primary and secondary sources, as we have seen previously. In past chapters, we also learned how to store the bibliographic information from your sources, e.g., using bibliographic referencing tools such as Zotero. And we partly examined how to take notes on sources and what information to look for when you analyze sources to support your argument. Now, in this chapter, we will learn how to cite information from our sources when we write our reports. First, we will look at *when* to cite sources. Second, we will examine *how* to cite sources.

2) When to cite sources

Simply put, we need to cite a source when we use it to get information from our paper. Specifically, there are four ways we can use information: A) direct quotation, B) indirect quotation, C) general reference, and D) adding additional information to the discussion. Let's look at each one of these in more detail.

A) Direct quotation

A direct quotation is when we directly quote a passage from a text, interview, or conversation. So, for example, imagine that you are reading an academic article about the importance of daily exercise. In this imaginary article, an "expert," Doctor Laura Smith, says that it is important to get at least thirty minutes of aerobic exercise every day. Perhaps this is a very important and convincing quote for your paper, and so you decide to quote it directly. In that case, you would write as follows:

> Doctor Laura Smith said that "it is important to get at least thirty minutes of aerobic exercise every day."

And, in this case, of course, after the direct quotation you would need to cite your source as well. That means that you would include information on title, author, and date of publication of the article that you took the quote from.

B) Indirect quotation

But, now let's imagine that you do not want to use a direct quotation. All you really want to do is state the main point of Doctor Laura Smith's comment without referring to her directly. After all, the information in the above quote is rather commonsensical. So, in that case, you could use an indirect quotation, such as follows:

> Experts agree that we should do a minimum of thirty minutes of aerobic exercise daily.

Now, we have used the exact same information from the above text and as in the first direct quotation, but we have done so in a way that doesn't directly use Doctor Laura Smith's words. So, this is called an indirect quotation.

C) General reference

But maybe you want to be even more general or reference some general fact or information without drawing your reader's attention to it in detail. For example, maybe you just want to state a fact which is already quite evident and do so in a general way. In this case, you can use a citation just as a general reference. Taking the same example as above, let's imagine that you just want to emphasize the importance of aerobic exercise without going into detail but at the same time point your reader in the direction of further studies on the subject. In that case, you could write something as follows:

Aerobic exercise is fundamental for healthy living.

Ok, that is pretty general right? You could actually just state this without a citation probably. But perhaps you want to provide evidence that what you are saying is true. In that case, especially, you could put a citation after the above sentence linking to Doctor Laura Smith's research article.

D) Adding additional information or discussion

Now, suppose you are writing about a topic or subject. You come across some really interesting research. You want to include it in your paper, but unfortunately you just cannot find a suitable place to put it in the body of the text. Or maybe even you are writing some sentences, but then you later realize that they are not totally relevant to your main discussion. You want to direct your reader's attention to this prior research or inform them of your additional information and discussion, but do so in a way that doesn't interrupt the flow of the main text body. What do you do? One way is to write the extra information in a *footnote*. A footnote is a note indicated by a number in the main text that goes at the bottom of the page. In Japanese, this is called 脚注 . History writers especially love to use footnotes because they come across lots of interesting historical facts in their research but which are not always directly relevant to their main point. Some examples of additional information that you could footnote are as follows:[10]

Footnote in the main text body
reshaping it to fit their aims and working it into their biographical identities. For these groups, the 16th Division garrison was a 'site of memory (*lieux de mémoire*)', based largely on positive – and highly localized and bordered – interpretations of the past, and which functioned to reaffirm and solidify group identity and narratives of self.[3] Yet as the Asia-

---

Figure 54: An image showing a footnote reference, indicated by the small number "3," in the text body of a research paper. Example is from author's forthcoming research publication "At the Border of Memory and History: Kyoto's Contested War Heritage," In Edward Boyle (ed). *Heritage, Conflicted Sites and Bordered Memories in Asia*, Brill (forthcoming 2022).

---

[10] The following examples are all from the author's forthcoming research publication, "At the Border of Memory and History: Kyoto's Contested War Heritage," In Edward Boyle (ed). *Heritage, Conflicted Sites and Bordered Memories in Asia*, Brill (forthcoming 2022).

Footnote at the bottom of the page

³ The term 'site of memory' is from Pierre Nora. Nora described history and memory as being in an antagonistic relationship. Memory on the one hand reaffirms and forms the basis for self and group identity. History on the other hand threatens to destroy memory by writing a history of memory. The combination of multiple group memories into history, in other words, undermines any single memory group's claims to individual ownership of the past. This reading of Nora's concept forms the foundational theoretical framework on which this paper's argument rests (Nora 1989). The idea of 'borders of memory' comes from Edward Boyle who explained heritage sites as bordered spaces where various mnemonic groups interact (Boyle 2019).

Figure 55: An image showing a footnote at the bottom of the page. Example is from author's forthcoming research publication "At the Border of Memory and History: Kyoto's Contested War Heritage," In Edward Boyle (ed). *Heritage, Conflicted Sites and Bordered Memories in Asia*, Brill (forthcoming 2022).

In the above example of a research paper that I wrote on the Kyoto 16th Division history, I used a footnote to talk about the term "site of memory." I did not want to discuss the meaning of the term in the main text because I thought it would distract the reader's attention. But it *is* an important term that is indirectly essential to my paper. Furthermore, "site of memory" is not *my* term: I was borrowing it from previous research, in this case that of Pierre Nora. So, I wanted to indicate to my readers that this is not my term. And, I also wanted to direct their attention to Nora's work so that they could reference it later. This was perfect additional information to include in a footnote.

Footnotes together on the larger page

including veterans and war bereaved groups, as well as the garrison's main postwar inheritor, a catholic Women's school called Seibo Jogakuin, laid stake to the garrison, reshaping it to fit their aims and working it into their biographical identities. For these groups, the 16th Division garrison was a 'site of memory (lieux de mémoire)', based largely on positive – and highly localized and bordered – interpretations of the past, and which functioned to reaffirm and solidify group identity and narratives of self.³ Yet as the Asia-Pacific War moved from memory to history, so too did its tangible relics. Later generations of historians and activists from the 1980s sought to clarify the historical significance of the garrison by synthesizing the narratives of multiple memory groups into a critical history of the site. But this undermined previous memory groups' exclusive claims to ownership of the past at the garrison. Moreover, activist-historian's attempts to construct a more cosmopolitan memory by uncovering and confronting painful events from the garrison's past such as the Nanking Massacre, and by including voices of Asian victims of Japanese militarism and the 16th Division in their accounts, drew fierce opposition from the garrison's other stakeholders. The garrison's partial designation as a Cultural Property, Japan's version of cultural heritage, in 2016 seemed to provide no solution to this impasse, either: the 16th Division garrison had become stuck at the border of history and memory. This essay examines how this situation came about, beginning with an overview of the 16th Division garrison's history, continuing through its postwar transformation into a bordered site of memory, and finally concluding with the return of history and the ensuing contestation this has engendered.

Footnotes together on the larger page

A History of the 16ᵗʰ Division Garrison

Part of the reason for the problematic nature of history and memory at the 16ᵗʰ Division garrison has to do with its function as a military base. Military bases are by nature liminal spaces. They are deeply intertwined with their surrounding local communities, often even becoming critical parts of regional economies and identities. Yet for the individual troops who train there, they are transitional places where a short period of months is spent before being deployed. At the same time, military bases become entangled in foreign affairs when troops are dispatched to conduct missions abroad. Military bases therefore interact with the local, national, and global on multiple levels, and they host diverse memory communities (e.g. soldiers and community members) in the process.⁴ Concurrently, military bases can become highly contested over the issue of whose memories and histories to emphasize there. Individual memory groups may attempt to write their own histories. But insofar as they fail to account for military bases' multidimensional aspects, they are likely to remain incomplete.

The 16ᵗʰ Division was no different. The Division was stationed in Kyoto's Fukakusa-mura (present-day Fushimi Ward, and a stone's throw away from the famous Fushimi Inari Shrine)

---

³ The term 'site of memory' is from Pierre Nora. Nora described history and memory as being in an antagonistic relationship. Memory on the one hand reaffirms and forms the basis for self and group identity. History on the other hand threatens to destroy memory by writing a history of memory. The combination of multiple group memories into history, in other words, undermines any single memory group's claims to individual ownership of the past. This reading of Nora's concept forms the foundational theoretical framework on which this paper's argument rests (Nora 1989). The idea of 'borders of memory' comes from Edward Boyle who explained heritage sites as bordered spaces where various mnemonic groups interact (Boyle 2019).

⁴ For an excellent history of how local, national, and international forces intersect in the space of military bases see Lutz 2001.

Figure 56: An image showing a full page from of a research paper with footnotes. Example is from author's forthcoming research publication "At the Border of Memory and History: Kyoto's Contested War Heritage," In Edward Boyle (ed). *Heritage, Conflicted Sites and Bordered Memories in Asia*, Brill (forthcoming 2022).

3) How to cite sources

There are multiple ways to cite sources. Each of these partly depends on which style you are using: Chicago, Harvard, Modern Language Association (MLA), etc. In this section, we will look at two referencing styles, Chicago and Harvard. I will then show two examples of how to use each of these styles. First, with the Chicago style, we will look at how to use footnotes. Second, with the Harvard style we will look at how to use in-text citations. In academic writing, both of these are frequently employed. Most often which one you use will depend on the instructor's preferences or the preferences of the journal or publisher you are working with. If you do not receive any specific instructions, you can pick one of your choosing. The important thing, however, is that you *do cite your sources* and that you *remain consistent* with your citation style. Typically, I recommend the Chicago style with footnotes.

A) Chicago style with footnotes

In the Chicago style with footnotes, each time we cite information (direct or indirect quote, general reference, additional information) we insert a footnote directly after the sentence. This inserts a small number. In Microsoft Word, this is easy to do with the following steps:

At the top of the page, click "references" and then "insert footnote."

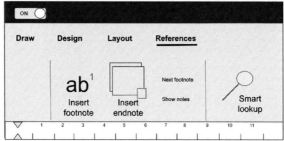

Figure 57: The author's rendition of where to find the "Insert footnote" tab in a recent version of Microsoft Word.

This adds a small number behind your sentence such as follows:

Doctor Laura Smith said that "it is important to get at least thirty minutes of aerobic exercise every day."[11)]

Then, in the footnote, at the bottom of the page, you should write the following information:

Book: Author's name, *Title* (Place of publication: Publisher name, Date), Page numbers

→ Book example: Zadie Smith, *Swing Time* (New York: Penguin Press, 2016), 315–16.

---

11) Laura Smith, "The Importance of Aerobic Exercise," *Fitness* Vol. 3, Issue 21 (April 2020): 13-30.

Journal: Author's name, "Title," *Journal name*, Volume, Number (Date): Page numbers.

→ Journal example: Susan Satterfield, "Livy and the Pax Deum," *Classical Philology* 111, no. 2 (April 2016): 170.

Note that you also need to list this same bibliographic information in your works cited page. We discussed partly how to do this in a previous chapter.

In the above, we have now seen how to use Chicago style footnotes for books and journal articles. But what about other kinds of sources? What about web pages? Or archival documents? In fact, there is a slightly different way to write each one of these. There is not time to go over all these in detail now. For further details, please consult the Chicago Manual of Style.

B) Harvard style in-text citations

Another common way to cite sources is with in-text citations. One popular style for this is the Harvard style. An example of how to use Harvard style in-text citations is as follows:

Experts agree that we should do a minimum of thirty minutes of aerobic exercise daily (Smith, 2020, p.15).

As you can see, in-text citations include: (Author's last name, date, page number). Note that it is not the author's full name but just the last name. Also, you include the page number from which you obtained this information. If you cite from the same source multiple times, you need to include an in-text citation each time and for different page numbers.

Additionally, if you already state the author's name in your sentence, such as is common in direct quotations like that below...

Doctor Laura Smith said that "it is important to get at least thirty minutes of aerobic exercise every day" (2020, p.15).

...then you do not need to write the author's name in your in-text citation. Note also that with in-text citations you do not need to write bibliographic information at the bottom of the page; you can just save all of this for the final works cited page.

4) Conclusion

Ok, so there you have it. That is the basic gist of how to cite sources. You now know A) when to cite sources and B) how to cite sources, and are familiar with two different citation styles: Chicago style with footnotes and Harvard style with in-text citations. You are well on your way to completing your research paper!

> **TRY:**
> ❑ Write citations for some two sources that you plan to use in your research. Practice using both Chicago style with footnotes and Harvard style with in-text citations for each one. Submit them to the instructor when you're finished.

CHAPTER TWELVE
Making a presentation

1) Introduction

In this chapter, we will learn some strategies for making great presentations. After you have completed your research report, you will often be asked to make a presentation to the class to summarize and to introduce your findings. But wait a minute, oh no! You mean we have to stand in front of the class and...talk. Ugh. That does not sound like fun at all. And with everyone watching our every move? How embarrassing. If this is how you feel, you are not alone. Many people find it difficult to talk in front of large crowds including and sometimes especially our peers. But have no fear. Armed with the right presentation strategies, there is in fact nothing at all to be afraid of. Once you know how to do it and have had practice doing it, talking in front of people becomes easy. Now, you do not have to be the most dynamic speaker in the world. We are not aiming for TED Talks here. Instead, this chapter just focuses on equipping you with the skills you will need to make an *effective* academic presentation and not to have to worry or become nervous about doing it. So, let's dive in.

2) Getting prepared

When getting ready for your presentation, one of the first things you will want to check is that you have your written report *already finished*. Now, given various time constraints, I realize that this may not always be possible or even feasible. But by the time you are ready to start presenting about your material, you should at least have some *idea* of your completed research project from start to finish, even if you are not yet done writing all the details.

The reason you want to have your written report basically finished is because, when you make your presentation, it will be helpful to use this as your guide. Of course, you *should not* read directly from your written report. This would likely be way too long. On top of this, written English and spoken English are generally two different things and employ different registers etc. Instead, you want to go through your written report and pull out all the key phrases, arguments, examples, and research findings, i.e., your conclusions. Sometimes it helps to go through with a pen or a highlighter and mark all the passages that you want to use in your presentation.

An important thing to remember is that your oral presentation should generally be *much shorter* than your written report. Time is limited, usually just to fifteen or twenty minutes, sometimes less, in oral presentations. You need to find your most important pieces of information and examples *only* and present these in an easy-to-understand way for your audience. It should be short and sweet.

Once you have done this, you are ready to move on to the next step. From here, the next thing you will generally want to do is to start making a PowerPoint slideshow to go along with your presentation.[12] You could also write a special written script to read aloud from for your oral presentation. This is especially helpful for very important speeches or academic presentations. However, it is not always necessary. I will go over the details and important characteristics of making a written script later in this section. But regardless of whether you have a written script or not, you will still most likely need to make a PowerPoint presentation or have some other visuals. So, let's look at some strategies for doing this next.

3) Making your PowerPoint slides

The most important things to be aware of when making PowerPoint slides are A) length and B) format. In this section, I will introduce a simple strategy for approaching these two points.

---

12) Note, I say "PowerPoint" here generally to refer to all kinds of PC slide-show format presentations rather than to indicate one particular software program. You may use whichever specific software program you are comfortable with.

First, regarding length, the general rule to keep in mind is that you should spend an average of two minutes per slide. Now, there are of course exceptions to this rule. Sometimes you need to move more quickly through slides or, other times, you may want to spend more time on a certain slide. But, in general, two minutes per slide is a good average length to begin with. Why? Well, put simply, it is difficult for people sitting in the audience to read a slide with lots of words on it in less than two minutes. This is especially true for larger rooms and for people sitting far in the back. Of course, you should not have too many words on your slide in the first place. But even with images or graphs, too, it is difficult to really get the message across on a visual level in less than two minutes. You want your slides and images to stick with people and have your audience remember your message. And to do this, you need two minutes per slide.

So, let's say, now, that you have an allotted time of fifteen minutes to make your presentation. Ok, so, fifteen divided by two is…roughly seven or eight. This means that you can make about seven or eight contents slides in your presentation. "Contents slides" means all the slides that you make that have information on them and which do not include your title slide or final bibliography slide. This gives you a general estimate for how long to make your PowerPoint.

The second thing to consider is format. Below is a simple example of how to generally format your PowerPoint slides in your presentation. Keep in mind, though, that this is a general guideline and not a hard rule, per se.

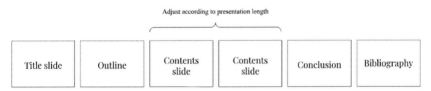

Figure 58: A simple model of how to compose PowerPoint (or other software) slides to accompany an oral presentation. Composed by Justin Aukema, 2022.

The first slide you want to include in your presentation is your title slide. This should give, for example, the title of your presentation, your name and affiliation, the date, and the name of the venue or class you are presenting in, if it is available. Below is an example of a title slide from a presentation I conducted on November 27, 2021, at Osaka City (Currently Metropolitan) University. The contents of the presentation were about Japan's *gokoku* shrines. You can see that

I include the title in large letters. This is especially something you want to have stick with your audience, so big is good. I also include my name and affiliation, although I did not put the date on this slide. Incidentally, the background image is a scan of an old postcard of Nara Gokoku Shrine from circa 1942. The postcard is in my personal collection, which means that obtaining separate copyright permissions is generally not an issue. It is often a good idea to have a visual on your title slide; something that conveys the general message of your presentation to the audience in one quick image. In my case, my presentation was about *gokoku* shrines, so I had an image of one of these shrines front and center on my first slide.

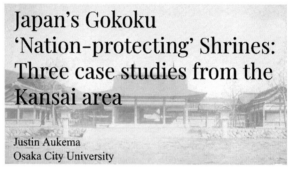

Figure 59: An image of the title page slide from a presentation conducted by the author in 2021.

After your title slide, you should have an outline slide. This is one slide usually written in bullet points that tells the audience simply and quickly what kind of information you are going to cover in your oral presentation. It should *not* be an outline of all the contents of your research report. Rather, it should be a simple outline of the contents *just of your talk*. So, along with this, you can say things like "in this talk, I will talk about…," and then go through the general order, i.e., "first, I will cover…," and "next, I will look at…." etc.

The next slides after this are your most important ones. These are your contents slides. This is where you summarize the information from your research report. As we have already discussed, you want to spend about two minutes per slide, especially in this section. So, you will want to adjust the number of your contents slides according to the overall allotted amount of time you have for your presentation. A fifteen-minute presentation would usually have between five to seven contents slides. This is because you can often spend less time on your title or bibliography slides.

Lastly, regarding the format of your presentation, you should have a conclusion slide and a bibliography slide at the very end. In your conclusion slide, you should simply summarize the conclusions from your oral presentation. You may also want to throw in some extra conclusions from your research report, even if you were not able to fully cover them in your presentation. You might also indicate some future avenues for research or remaining questions. Or you could draw some more speculative conclusions or tentative answers that the findings of your research hint at but may not prove definitively. The bibliography slide should simply include all the bibliographic references, that is to say source materials, that you used in compiling your oral presentation. Pictures, images, and graphs also often need bibliographic citations, so make sure to include these as well.

4) Making meaningful contents slides

Now that you have an idea of the general format of your PowerPoint presentation, let's look at some more specific strategies for how to make a meaningful and effective presentation. The most important aspect to focus on in this regard will be how to make your contents slides. There are many ways to make effective contents slides depending on what your topic or research field is and what kind of presentation you want to make. Below, I will explain some strategies to help you make powerful contents slides. Keep in mind, of course, that this is not an exhaustive list.

A) Use of visuals (pictures and images): Perhaps one of the best things to include in your PowerPoint presentation is visuals such as pictures and images. These could be pictures that you took, or that you found somewhere else. In the first case, you will often be free to use the images however you want. Some of the best visual sources you can use are images that you have made or photographs that you have taken. However, many times we will want to use images that belong to someone else. For purposes of classroom oral presentations, a simple bibliographic citation is usually enough in these cases. But for some larger presentations, or if you intend to publish your work, you will also likely need to get copyright permission to use the image. I cannot cover the detailed process of copyright permission here. But the best place to start for this is to contact the organization that made the image or the research institution (e.g., a museum) where you found the image.

Images are important especially because you can let them do the talking for you. Usually, you should not have too many words in your PowerPoint presentation. You will want to have some key phrases, terms, and findings typed out on your slides. But other than this, you want to have your words be the part that you *say aloud* and the PowerPoint be the part that you *show visually* to your audience. So, images are usually better than words in most cases. The images should, however, directly relate to and *support* what you are talking about as you give your presentation.

Below is an example of an image slide that I used in a presentation. The image is from a source we have already discussed, the 1936 *Manshū haken kinen shashin-cho*. This source is important because it demonstrates some of the Kyoto 16th Division's daily activities during their deployment to Japanese-occupied Manchuria in 1936. I used this image because it shows visual evidence that Japanese forces burned villages there in an attempt to crush opposition and resistance. As you can see, there are very few words on the slide, only the title of the publication where I found the image. This image is a scan of a source, a book, as mentioned. I found this book in archives in Kyoto and was able to use the image in my presentation without dealing with copyright. However, in advance of using the image for publication, I needed to obtain permission from the specific museum.

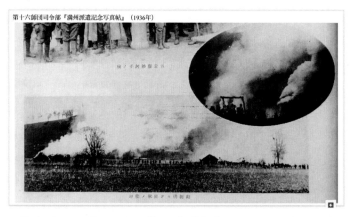

Figure 60: An image of a contents (image) slide from a presentation conducted by the author in 2020. The image is from Daijūroku Shidan Shireibu (ed.). *Manshū haken kinen shashin-chō*. Kyoto: Daijūroku Shidan Shireibu, 1936. Kyoto Institute, Library and Archives, Serial Number KO 396.9 D19, Material ID 110296549.

B) <u>Explanation of sources</u>: Another type of contents slide you may wish to make is an explanation or analysis of some of the main sources that you used in your research. In historical research, evidence comes almost entirely in the form of old documents, articles, or diary entries, etc. Much of historian's arguments and analysis are themselves based entirely on an analysis and discussion of the various sources that they uncovered during their research. There is an old idea in the field of history that the historian is letting the sources "speak for themselves." While this kind of empiricism has been criticized, many times rightly so, it is also undeniable that primary sources and source analysis especially remain very important for historical research. So, simply introducing these sources to the audience is one of the most meaningful kinds of contents slides that we can make in our oral presentations.

Below is an example a source analysis slide that I made for my presentation on *gokoku* shrines. The source in question is a 1939 article on *gokoku* shrines published by the Home Ministry (Naimushō) in the government organ magazine *Shūhō*. I found this source at the National Diet Library. The source was highly important for me since it described why the government was establishing *gokoku* shrines as a separate category, but which were also closely related to the Yasukuni Shrine in Tokyo.

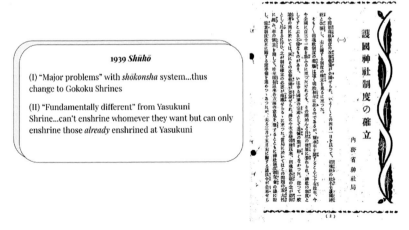

Figure 61: An image of a source analysis slide from a presentation conducted by the author in 2021. The source is Naimushō Jinja-kyoku, "Gokoku jinja seido no kakuritsu," *Shūhō*, No. 131 (April 1939): 2-8.

Another type of source analysis you may wish to do that is similar to this is a quick review of key works of secondary literature that you read. This may be important if some of this secondary literature is crucial for understanding your topic, or if you focus on critiquing previous views in scholarship through your research. In this case, you might want to show an image of the book cover in question along with your critique or analysis of it to one side.

C) Newspaper images and analysis: Old newspapers are a rich source of information about the past. In many cases, even just the headlines alone can be quite revealing and leave a lasting impression. A good strategy for historians, therefore, can be to take image scans of these newspapers and to paste them directly into your presentation.

Figure 62: An image of a newspaper slide from a presentation by the author conducted in 2021. The newspaper articles are variously dated 1929-1944 from the *Kyōtō Hinode Shinbun*.

Above is an example of a newspaper slide that I made for a presentation on the Kyoto 16th Division history. We have already discussed the contents of this research and seen some of these news articles previously, so I will not go into too much detail about them here. But simply notice how I have taken image scans of the articles or their headlines and nothing more. These articles supported the contents of my oral presentation and left a powerful and quick impression with the audience.

D) <u>Quotes from sources:</u> Similar to source analysis is using direct quotes
from one of your primary or secondary sources. This is not always
recommended, since quotations inevitably require lots of words, and,
in general, it is not good to have *too many* words on your slides. But
in certain cases, it is simply impossible to convey the message you
want to convey without using a direct quote. If you are going to read a
long passage in your oral presentation especially then you may want to
simultaneously show this quote on the screen to the audience, since it
may be difficult just to follow along. In written languages like Japanese,
especially, this is dually important, because very often quotations use
difficult or antiquated Chinese characters or other forms of writing that
would be difficult to decipher without seeing.

Figure 63: An image of a quotation slide from a presentation conducted by the author in 2021. The source is Kutsuma Yasuji, Kyoto Shimbun-sha (eds.),
Sakimori no shi, (Kyoto: Kyoto Shimbun, 1976-1994).

Above is an example of a quotation slide that I made for the 1981
book *Sakimori no shi* by Kutsuma Yasuji. This slide was also from my
presentation on the Kyoto 16th Division. This book was an important
primary source for me, since it demonstrated the shifting historical
consciousness surrounding the 16th Division. I wanted to indicate this
source and a quote from it to demonstrate how it was different from
previous sources up to that time. In my presentation, I used an actual
image of the book cover. However, I have replaced this with a generic
representation of it due to copyright issues here.

E) <u>Data and graphs:</u> For social scientists, graphs and numerical data or statistics are also usually essential. This could include wage or price indices, demographic information, or other statistics. The graphs can be simple, such as just a table of dates and information. Or of course they could be more complex graphs utilizing large data sets and illustrating them with bar, pie, scatter, or other graphs.

When we use graphs, we will also want to spend some time talking about them. Graphs and data are somewhat different in this respect from the other contents slides I have introduced so far. Previously, we saw how slides with visuals for example can be used to illustrate or to support the contents of our presentation. But with graphs and data, we will often want to spend more time on these because they directly show the points we are talking about. When talking about graphs and data, the following phrases may come in handy.

 Speak!

"This graph shows that..."
"As you can see from the graph..."
"The x/y axis displays..."
"The [COLOR] line/bar/section indicates..."

Next, let's look at some examples of how to use these phrases together with graphs. The two graphs and tables below are ones that I have made and used in my own research and class teaching.

EXAMPLE 1

Top 20 IMF borrowers by outstanding credit (in billions of USD)

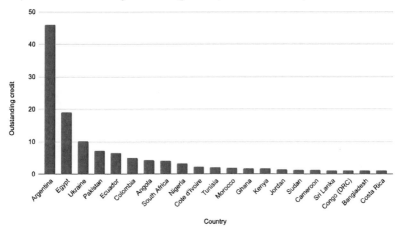

 "This graph shows the top 20 borrowers to the IMF by outstanding credit in billions of US dollars. As you can see from the graph, countries like Argentina, Egypt, and Ukraine are the top borrowers. The x axis shows the names of the countries, and the y axis shows the amount of outstanding debt."

Figure 64: A bar graph showing the top borrowers from the IMF as of 2022 in billions of US dollars. Composed by Justin Aukema, 2022. Based on data from IMF, "Total IMF Credit Outstanding," August 22, https://www.imf.org/external/np/fin/tad/balmov2.aspx?type=TOTAL and converted from SDRs to USD based on the chart at IMF, "SDR Valuation," https://www.imf.org/external/np/fin/data/rms_sdrv.aspx.

EXAMPLE 2

Rise in wages vs rise in prices, 1995 - 2020

	Nominal wages	Prices
Korea	2.92x	1.92x
U.S.	2.23x	1.7x
England	2.08x	1.64x
Germany	1.64x	1.41x
Japan	0.96x	1.04x

Data compiled by Ueno Takeshi, NLI Research Institute

"This table shows the rise in wages versus the rise in prices between 1995 and 2020 in various countries. The left column lists each country; the middle column shows the rise in nominal wages; and the right column shows the rise in prices. Japan is at the very bottom. As you can see, whereas in other countries wages have risen faster than prices, in Japan, the opposite is true: prices have risen more than wages."

Figure 65: A table comparing the rise in wages versus the rise in prices in various countries including Japan between 1995 and 2020. Composed by Justin Aukema, 2022. Based on data compiled by Ueno Takeshi from the NLI Research Institute. Adapted from a similar table in "Agaranai chingin 'Nihon dake ga ijō,' motomerareru seisaku no kenshō," *Tōkyō Shimbun*, June 15, 2022, https://www.tokyo-np.co.jp/article/183402.

Now you know some strategies for making meaningful contents slides in your oral presentation. Of course, there are other effective ways to make PowerPoint slides, too. But with the above list, you should be well on your way toward making a powerful presentation.

5) Using a written script

Now, I mentioned before that you may also want to read from a written script when you conduct your presentation. There is no single or *right* way to make a presentation. But there are some advantages and disadvantages to using or not using a written script.

Pros and cons of using a written script

Pros	Cons
• Easier to relax during presentation • Can cover more information • Can more precisely time your presentation • Can use the written script later	• Might sound too formal to the audience • Harder to deviate from the script and/or include new information • Very hard to adjust if you accidentally go over time

Figure 66: A table comparing the pros and cons of using a written script in an oral presentation. Composed by Justin Aukema, 2022.

First the pros. If you do decide to make a written script, you already have all the work done before your big presentation. This can be a huge relief and weight off your shoulders, especially if you tend to be nervous or if the presentation venue is very big and/or formal. Reading from a script is much easier than reading without a script in this regard. Also, you can cover more information typically when reading from a script. When we speak off the cuff, we tend to use lots of "ahs" and "ums." But with a written script, all this extraneous material is cut out, and we can get right to the point. This also relates to timing. If your script is well timed, reading from a script can be much easier than going without. The general rule for timing is this: **it takes two minutes to read one full page, double-spaced**. Furthermore, if you are reading in a second language, it will probably take longer than this. I would plan for **three minutes to read one page** in a foreign language. Based on this, if you have a fifteen-minute presentation, your presentation script should be about seven pages long. Another benefit of using a written script is that you can use it again later. You will always have a record of your presentation, and you might choose to publish this somewhere else in the future or to develop it into a future journal article.

However, there are also some cons to using a written script. One is that they are typically not as dynamic or impactful for the listener. Powerful speeches are usually practiced well in advance and nearly memorized. They may also include elements of spontaneity. But these things are hard to do with a written script. With a written script, it will be hard to escape the sense that you are reading aloud to the audience, and, furthermore, it is difficult in this regard to escape formal sounding written language. In addition, if you need to change or modify your oral presentation on the fly, it will be very hard to do this with a written script. It is difficult to deviate from something that you have typed up in front of you. This also relates to timing. If you do not time your written script well, then there is a danger that you could have a script that is *too long*. If this happens, you are in trouble, because you will need to skip large sections of your writing. And since you have not left much wiggle room for maneuverability, it will be challenging to squeeze in the necessary information on the go.

These pros and cons will give you a rough idea of which way you might want to go with your oral presentation. Generally, though, I like to go with a written script. This is because I do not have a natural-born talent for rhetoric and speech making. I tend to stumble around with my words and to go off on tangents. I also often get nervous, especially when speaking in second languages. That is why I feel much more comfortable reading from a script that I have prepared. But you may feel differently. Especially if you have a good grasp of the material and feel very confident, you may choose to go without a written script instead.

6) Fielding questions

Ok, so let's imagine this: your presentation is over. You have successfully laid out your arguments and all without tripping over your tongue too much. You are pretty proud of yourself: as you should be. Congratulations! But, then someone in the audience raises their hand and asks you a question. Maybe you are lucky and it is a question that you can answer easily and off the top of your head. But most questions actually do not work that way. Most of the time, audience members' questions are about aspects of our topic that *we have not yet considered*. If the question is relevant then this could actually be the best type of question because it helps us develop our future research. But still up there at the podium, you are stuck with this question; you have no script, and you have no idea how to answer. What do you do? Basically there is a set strategy for how to deal with this. Just follow the steps below:

(A) First, respond by saying something like…

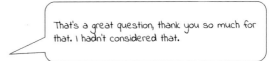

That's a great question, thank you so much for that. I hadn't considered that.

(B) Next, you want to shift the conversation, and the question, away from a topic you don't know much about and toward a topic that *you do* know something about. You might say something like…

In fact, when I was researching, I didn't come across much information about that. However, I did find out information all about…[new related topic].

(C) Or maybe you *did* find relevant information related to the question, you just didn't have time to mention it in your main presentation.

Yes, thank you, that's a great question. In fact, I did find out some really interesting information about that. [Explain]

(D) Either way, the goal (for you) of question and answer time is to *present new information* that you did not have time to discuss in your main presentation. So, if the question does not directly relate to this, you need to subtly change the conversation to the topic that you want. And if the question does relate to this, then great, you are all set! Summarized, then, the basic rule of question and answer is this: <u>"don't answer the question you got, answer the question you wanted."</u>

7) Conclusion

In this chapter, we have learned some helpful strategies for making effective oral presentations. In particular, we focused on practical and concrete steps such as what kind of slides and information to include in a PowerPoint presentation. Even if you are not naturally blessed with the gift of rhetoric (don't worry, not many of us are!), you do not need to worry. Like many things in life, almost anything, presentations included, are mostly an acquired skill. With patience, practice, and the right tools they can be learned and even perfected. For some pre-presentation practice, try completing the following tasks with a classmate.

TRY:
- [ ] Use one of the sources you have found and practice making a simple contents slide for your presentation. When you are finished, show and talk about your example slide to the class.

TRY:
- [ ] Do you use graphs or charts in your presentation or paper? If so, practice talking about them using the methods described above with a partner.

Part II
Critical Thinking Skills

CHAPTER THIRTEEN
Understanding "bias" in science

---

1) Introduction

Now, I know what you are probably thinking: science is not biased...right? Well, the short answer is "wrong." Science, like any other human system, is not infallable. And it is not free from bias either. People who practice science, or scientists, are living, breathing people. They are deeply embedded in their social systems, institutions, and historical contexts. They are partially products of their own environments. And they are subject to political and other kinds of pressures just like anyone else. So, yes, science, or what we think of as science, is absolutely biased. But, guess what? Fortunately for us science and critical thought also present a way out of the paradox by which it is bound. In other words, it is possible to see through bias, even the deepest kind of bias embedded in science, with science itself.

2) What is "science" anyway?

But wait a minute, you might say, how is that possible? Well, it all comes down to the nature of *what* science is. Many people have a mistaken impression of science. They think that science is when experts tell them things, and then if they believe those experts, they are acting scientifically. Sadly, this is actually a very *unscientific* way to approach science. Just because someone has an advanced degree or is in a position of power, does not mean that they are always right. Nor do they have a monopoly on knowledge.

Ok, so what *is* science, then? The Merriam-Webster Dictionary defines it partly as follows: science is…

> **Science…**
> "…knowledge or a system of knowledge covering general truths or the operation of general laws especially as obtained and tested through scientific method" (Merriam-Webster, 2022).

Hmm, "system of knowledge," "general truths…," this all sounds pretty vague. But wait a minute, the "scientific method"? What is that? In fact, the scientific method is key to understanding what science really is. The scientific method has been used for centuries since the Enlightenment. It is a simple, often six-step, process that centers around the importance of doubt and skepticism. The point is not to just believe what you are told but rather to begin from a position of *skepticism*. Instead of belief, the scientific method is a process that advocates asking questions and rigorously testing hypothesis with experiments to obtain results. It can be thought of as follows:

> **The Scientific Method**
>
> 1) Make an observation and/or ask a question
> 2) Research the topic area
> 3) Form a hypothesis
> 4) Test with experiments
> 5) Analyze the data
> 6) Report your conclusions
> 7) *Repeat the process

Figure 67: A simple explanation of the scientific method.

The scientific method is key to understanding what science is. It is not a fixed or static thing; it is not something that so-called experts report to you. It is an active, ongoing process that anyone can do. And key to this process is starting from a position of doubt. Do not just believe what you are told. Go out and observe for yourself! And more importantly, test your observations, make hypotheses (informed guesses about why something happens or is the way it is), and test with experiments. What's more, even when you have collected some data or conducted an experiment, does this mean that you have arrived at the truth or at something factual? Well, maybe. But also, maybe not. Because the other essential point about the scientific method is that it never stops. One time is never enough. You must repeat your experiments, to see if they turn out the same way again. Or, in addition, other people need to test and confirm those same experiments, to see if they can arrive at the same results.

Only once something has been repeatedly confirmed through vigorous and multiple tests and experiments can it be thought of as scientific "fact." But still, some people or scientists may still have doubts about even these scientific facts. And guess what? That is ok, too. Baseless doubt is of course unscientific. But everyone is entitled to reasonable doubt, especially if it can form the basis for their further and ongoing experiments.

3) The importance of doubt and the problems of "fact"

But why is it so important to doubt? Wouldn't it just be easier if we uncritically accepted scientific facts that have been proven by experts? Well, yes, sure it would be *easier*. But it would not necessarily be *better*, nor would it necessarily add to the global totality of accumulated historical knowledge. Why? Because, simply put, even scientific "facts" often turn out to be wrong.

Don't believe me? Well then just think about some of the most famous examples of when the entire body of so-called scientific knowledge was forced to undergo a sea change and revise some of its most fundamental suppositions. For example, many scientists used to practice *phrenology*, which was the "science" of measuring people's skulls to determine their personality traits. This was practiced widely in the 19th century. But today, it is regarded as a false *pseudo-science*, or fake science. Or here is another example. For centuries, most educated and powerful people believed in the geocentric model of the solar system. This was the idea that the sun and all the planets rotated around the earth, i.e., that the earth was at the center of the universe. But then, in the 16th century, Nicolaus Copernicus discovered that it was the other way around: the planets revolved around the stationary sun! These are just some examples of how the entire body of scientific knowledge can change following a new discovery. Everything that so-called experts once thought was *absolutely right* can actually be proven, well…absolutely wrong. And that is why it is always healthy to maintain a small amount of criticism about even the most established scientific theories and facts.

Speaking of which, you know who else had something to say on this matter? The father of Western philosophy and science himself, Socrates. He was famously noted by Plato for claiming "I know that I know nothing." In other words, Socrates understood that the root of true wisdom was not massive amounts of accumulated knowledge, but rather the opposite. He knew that starting from a position of humility toward the universe was the best and most *scientific* position. Because think about it: if we already knew everything, then why would we need to conduct experiments and tests in the first place? Socrates' famous dictum is in fact similar to the common folk wisdom that "there's no such thing as a stupid question." The true mark of ignorance is not asking any questions in the first place.

4) The social foundations of science

Another important figure to shape our thinking about science was Karl Marx. He understood that people are products of the society and especially the *class* that they are born into. For instance, Marx famously said that even man's consciousness is not his own but is rather shaped by his socio-historical circumstances (and relations to the means of production, i.e., his class).[13] Marx also elaborated that religion, culture, politics, and yes, even science, are all subject by economic pressures and concerns. For instance, if in a given economic system it is regarded as normal or "natural" for people to work for money wages, then the religion, politics, and science of a society will also reflect this relationship. Put more simply, if money becomes the most basic expression of the fulfillment of social need, then money will influence politics, religion, and science. This is obvious for us today. Consider, for instance, that it is impossible to conduct academic or scientific research without large amounts of money, usually from private or public grants, funding, and scholarships. Only those with the requisite amount of money can go to higher education in the first place! And the orientation of science toward monetary goals will also affect what it takes as the subject of its research. So, for instance, scientific studies will tend to focus on developing "new" and "unique" products that can be bought and sold for a profit, rather than, say, repeated re-testing or questioning of established techniques for the free improvement of general society. On top of this, Marx

---

13) See, for example, the Preface to *A Contribution to the Critique of Political Economy*, 1859. Cited in Karl Marx and Friedrich Engels, *The Marx-Engels Reader*, Edited by Robert C. Tucker. 2nd Revised & Enlarged edition, (New York: W. W. Norton & Company, 1978), 4.

recognized that it is the ideology or ideas of the ruling class that are dominant in every age.[14] When applied to science and the ruling ideology of money (or capitalism) this means that it will usually be the powerful (those with money) who influence the direction of science, and not the vulnerable, the weak, or the poor.

In fact, Marx's ideas about science can be observably verified even without reading his voluminous works. This is evidenced in the powerful effect that money, politics, and prestige have over science. For example, remember Obokata Haruko? She was a researcher at the Riken Center for Developmental Biology who, in 2013, discovered what she called pluripotent stem cells. She claimed that this was when ordinary cells could be turned into embryonic stem cells (the building blocks of life) just by soaking them in slightly acidic water. Obokata's amazing "discovery" was published in the most prestigious science journal in the world, *Nature*, and were positively praised around the world and especially in the Japanese media. But there was just one small problem: her findings were completely false. She and her team had forged and falsified the data of their experiments. What's more, it was later discovered that she had plagiarized portions of her earlier work as well. The Obokata case illustrates some of the problems of contemporary science.[15] Researchers are under tremendous pressure to make amazing "new" discoveries mainly so they can advance their own careers. This is a further result of a capitalist system which privileges not only marketable discoveries, but also in which scientists themselves are required to produce such products to maintain their own existence.

---

14) From *The German Ideology*. Cited in Karl Marx and Friedrich Engels, *The Marx-Engels Reader*, Edited by Robert C. Tucker. 2nd Revised & Enlarged edition, (New York: W. W. Norton & Company, 1978), 172.
15) Sven Saaler made a similar argument in 2014. See Sven Saaler, "The Problems of Science Management: Riken Is No Isolated Case," *Nippon.com*, April 16, 2014, https://www.nippon.com/en/column/g00162/.

CHAPTER FOURTEEN
Reading the news

1) Introduction

In this chapter, we will learn simple ways to read the news. Now, you probably hear your other teachers say this all the time: "read the news." Ok, but why should we read the news? That is a question that is often left unanswered. Probably to help us get ideas for our own research topics, might be one answer, right? Or, also just to get a sense of what is "going on" in the world, perhaps? But then we are told something else: "beware of fake news." Uh…what? So, we should watch/read the news, but we should also beware of fake news. Now even I am getting confused. So, let me help set the record straight. We *should* read the news, but we should also be careful doing so. In this chapter, we will learn how to do this. Also, we should beware of fake news sure. But we should also keep in mind that the distinction between fake and real when it comes to the news is often hard to figure out. Part of the problem is that almost all news contains bias, exaggeration, and certain political perspectives and varying levels of accuracy. So, there is no clear distinction really between totally fake and totally trustworthy "real" news. We just need to be critical of all news all the time. This is not hard to do once we know how to do it. So, let's get started.

2) What is the news?

Part of the misunderstanding when it comes to news is that many people are not clear what "news" is in the first place. News does not operate on the same sets of rigorous scientific standards that we try to abide by in academia. When we operate scientifically, we form hypothesis and research questions, gather data and information, perform tests and experiments, and observe the results.

Then we report the results regardless of whether they affirmed or confirmed our initial hypothesis. Sometimes our tests and data might yield totally different results than we expected. Now, science is not perfect, either, as we saw in the last chapter. But the point is that, in theory, it is supposed to operate on a set of principles which are entirely different than those in the news. Sure, news-media has principles and standards, too. For instance, we have probably all heard the idea that news is supposed to be "objective" or to report "both" or "multiple" sides of any given event. I will explain more about the problems of this shortly.

For the time being, the important point to remember, though, is that news differs from science and scholarly study because it is not intended to be a careful, historical analysis of the events that it reports on. It simply reports current events as they are happening. It does not try to answer *why* those events or happening. Or, if it does do this, it does not do so with much historical depth. Moreover, news reporters do not conduct their own experiments to derive their own conclusions. Instead, they rely on so-called experts, pundits, or the voices of average people to gather and report a variety of opinions and viewpoints. Most news reporters themselves *do not know much about* the events they are reporting on. For example, most news reporters do not read big, long, scholarly books about the subjects they report on. But don't take my word for it. This is plainly obvious by comparing the differences between scholarly studies and news.

Scholarly works vs news

Scholarship	News
• Contains a unique finding or argument • Uses original data and experiments • Highlights historical analysis and context • Explains previous scholarship • Uses and cites many sources that are clearly labeled	• Reports current events • Relies on the views of "experts," pundits, or average people • No historical context • Doesn't explain prior scholarship • Does not cite sources

Figure 68: A table comparing scholarly works with the news. Composed by Justin Aukema, 2022.

Now, these are just some examples. It is not a complete list of differences, and it is probably a bit of a simplification. But it gets the point across. I introduced some of the first differences already. So, I want to especially focus on the last three points. First, any scholarly work needs to explain how and why its findings and arguments are unique. To do this, it needs to briefly summarize the history of the problem and other scholars' findings about it. But news does not do this at all. It simply reports current events without going into detail about their history, why they are happening, or why they are important. The lack of historical consciousness is, in my opinion, the biggest problem with the news. For example, many times news-media will report something that totally contradicts something else that it reported months or years earlier. This is because news articles are not even aware of what *their own newspaper* has already reported in the past. Secondly, and most importantly, news-media does not cite sources. Many times, it does not even use sources. This means that it does not conduct research and is not independently verifiable. I know this from personal experience writing news articles. Newspapers do check sources. But they are usually personal interviews or other easily obtainable information. Moreover, when the newspaper editor checks the sources, he or she deletes the citation before printing the article. In the past I have cited books in my news articles. But this has caused problems with newspaper editors who prefer *not* to use books because they take too long to confirm the information in them.

So, we can already see that the news contains some serious problems. But I admit, I am not being totally fair to the news. This is because there is one other type of reporting that we also find in newspapers and on television sometimes that is different from the news. This is called *journalism*. Journalism is unique, in-depth reporting on a certain subject that often seeks to answer what causes events and to map their effects. Many times, journalists spend months and even years researching a topic and gathering information and data. The rigorous methods that they apply is less similar to news reporters and more similar to professional historians. In fact, many journalists, after reporting in newspapers, will go on to publish the rest of their findings in nonfiction or history books. Of course, journalism does face some of the same problems as news, though. For example, when published in newspapers, journalists still usually don't cite or print their sources. Moreover, they are still subject to problems of media bias, either on the part of the individual journalist or from the news company. But, overall, journalism is a much more important and useful source of information than simple news reporting.

5) The problem of "objectivity"

Now, some might protest my evaluation of the news. They might say, "but news-media *does* have standards because it strives for objectivity." Hmm, ok, objectivity. Well, it is certainly true that some journalists and reporters do try to be objective, or as objective as possible in their work. But the problem is that it is impossible for anyone to be truly objective. Moreover, not acknowledging this inherent limitation and simply giving the impression of truth or objectivity is highly *un-scientific* and very misleading, bordering on the point of outright lying. The reasons for this are easy to understand with some simple investigation of how society operates and what "objectivity" really is. Below, I will introduce four of the most basic issues: the problem of context, the problem of selection, the problem of bias, and the problem of propaganda.

The problem of context

First, we all live and grow up in specific contexts. We are not just individuals, but we are also members of society. And the society and contexts in which we grow up and live influence how we think and act. This includes all the groups we are a part of, where we go to school and work, and who are family is. We can visualize the individual in society as follows.

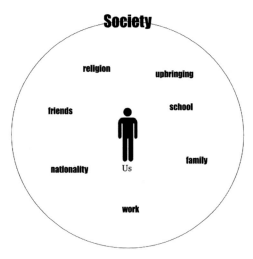

Figure 69: An image of the individual in society and the various social groups that influence our thinking. Composed by Justin Aukema, 2022.

The point is that these social groups not only influence how we think, but they also give us all our ideas, thoughts, and beliefs, too. This affects the entire way in which we see the world. This means that we never really see any event or phenomenon totally objectively, as a passive or totally outside observer would. Rather, we always see that thing, that event, through the social context of which we are a part. This is easily observable. People of different religions and nationalities often have totally different ways of explaining the world. And the reporting of news-media in different countries is often totally different. We can imagine the image of the person in the above visual as the news reporter, for instance, or ourselves as we watch the news. Either way, the point is that true objectivity anywhere, let alone news media, is already difficult because of these things.

The problem of selection

The other main problem regarding objectivity in news media is simply that it is impossible to report everything that happens in a single day. Consider the visual below.

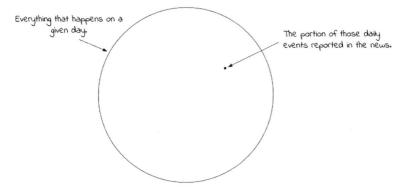

Everything that happens on a given day.

The portion of those daily events reported in the news.

Figure 70: An image illustrating the difficulty of achieving true "objectivity" in the news. Composed by Justin Aukema, 2022.

Lots of stuff happens every day. An *immense* amount actually. Babies are born, people die, fires start and are put out. But most of this is not reported in the news. And why not? Because it is simply physically impossible. No one would have the time or resources to report every drop of rain or every time a butterfly flaps its wings. Why is this important? Because it means that all news reporters everywhere *always make a choice* about what to report. They do not report everything equally since this would be impossible. So, they or their bosses at the news agency choose what is or is not "important." Many factors influence their selection. What topics will their readers be interested in? What topics will help them sell newspapers? What topics are they being *told* to report on? Whatever these individual factors may be, the problem of selection remains. But what is deemed "important" to a news company may not actually be important to our daily lives. Conversely, very important things may be happening in the world that *are never reported at all*. Most notably all kinds of social problems such as homelessness, poverty, starvation, and exploitation of the labor force are so taken for granted that they almost never appear in the news.

The problem of bias

Perhaps the biggest obstacle toward "objectivity," however, is that of bias. Everybody everywhere has bias. There are certain things we like and dislike; our decisions are influenced by our social groups and contexts; and we are pushed and pulled by political and even unconscious factors that influence our decision making. In news-media, the biggest problem regarding bias is the problem of ownership. News companies are *for profit* corporations. Their main goal is to sell papers and to make money and profit. This already influences what they report on and how they report it, since stories that seem like they will be popular and sell papers immediately take preference. Even so-called non-profit news agencies typically must receive grants from large institutions or corporations to stay afloat. The simple fact of the matter is that it costs money to run a news organization, and somebody's got to pay for it.

Moreover, much of the news media is owned and controlled by a few giant corporations and very rich people. In the United States, for example, fifteen billionaires and six corporations own most news outlets.[16] The world's richest person, Amazon CEO Jeff Bezos, for example owns the Washington Post, one of the most read and respected papers in America. Ironically, its tagline is "Democracy Dies in Darkness." This is despite the fact that the paper itself is owned by one person and not everyone equally, as the term "democracy" would imply. Even newswires like Reuters, for instance, are owned by various stockholders who influence decision making and what issues get reported and how. Some other quick examples include ABC News, which is owned by Disney; NBC, which is owned by Comcast; and Fox News, which is owned by

---

16) See Carly Hallman, "Who Owns Your News? The Top 100 Digital News Outlets and Their Ownership," *Titlemax*, https://www.titlemax.com/discovery-center/lifestyle/who-owns-your-news-the-top-100-digital-news-outlets-and-their-ownership/.

the Murdoch family.

In this situation, achieving "objectivity" in the news becomes somewhat laughable. Newspapers, for example, clearly do not want to do anything that would negatively impact both A. their bottom line and B. their stockholders' profits. This means that they must report things that are beneficial toward these aims and avoid topics that are either not profitable or which criticize or hurt their owners. It also means that many news outlets will either directly or indirectly support various political positions that are favorable to their owners.

The problem of propaganda

Now we arrive at the last problem of "objectivity." The issue is simply this: many times, the news is not only biased, but it is also *outright lies*. Lying is not an anomaly in the news; it is a part of what the news is, and it happens *all the time*. Ever since modern news was invented it has lied. For instance, so-called yellow journalism was common in the late 19th century. This was when news reports purposely exaggerated or used sensationalism to sell newspapers. It is sort of like click-bait today! And this had dangerous consequences. It helped drive the US and Spain to go to war in Cuba and the Philippines. Such sensationalism was a key part of early newspapers. William Randolph Hearst, who developed the United States' largest newspaper company in the early 20th century, routinely used exaggerated headlines and images to sell newspapers, eventually making him one of the most wealthy and powerful people in the country at the time.

News media lies also famously get worse during periods of conflict and wartime. Frequently this turns into propaganda. Some of the most famous photographs of Gettysburg during the U.S. Civil War (1861-65) were fabricated and/or exaggerated. This continued much later during WWI when all major belligerents utilized the news to distribute propaganda, so that they could influence people and motivate them to fight. Later, during the Spanish Civil War (1936-39), Robert Capa notoriously took one of the most famous war photographs ever taken and which was published and seen around the world, that of the "Falling Solider." It depicts a man getting shot in the heat of battle. The problem is that many now suspect it was likely a fake![17] During WWII, too, all sides used propaganda and lies in the news media to an unprecedented extent.

---

17) See, for example, Larry Rohter, "New Doubts Raised Over Famous War Photo," *The New York Times*, August 17, 2009, https://www.nytimes.com/2009/08/18/arts/design/18capa.html.

Newspapers in wartime Japan, for instance, were famously covered with lies. To cite just one example, in April 1942, 16 US B-25 medium bombers launched an air attack against Tokyo, killing fifty people and injuring 400 more. But Japanese newspapers did not report this at all. Instead, here is what the *Asahi Shimbun* wrote the following day:

> "Enemy planes attacked Tokyo today; 9 planes shot down; damage to the capital light" 「きょう帝都に敵機来襲　9機を撃墜、わが損害軽微」[18]

So, this is what people all around Japan read and believed. The problem? It was totally false. No American bombers were shot down and the damage to Tokyo was certainly not "light" as the headline suggested. And this is just one example of wartime propaganda during WWII. Throughout the war, the Japanese Imperial Headquarters 大本営 issued radio reports 大本営発表 that were reproduced in the news and which were notoriously false.

The list of wartime propaganda and media lies could go on and on, right up to the present. One of the supposed attacks in the 1964 Gulf of Tonkin Incident and which was used to escalate the Vietnam War never happened, even though it was reported in the news media. In 2003, US Secretary of State Colin Powell claimed in a presentation to the UN Security Council that Saddam Hussein possessed weapons of mass destruction and that, therefore, the US should attack Iraq. Even though this was later proven to be false, the US and much world media reported it as fact at the time. And in 2019, news outlets including the *New York Times*, CNN, and the BBC reported that the forces of Venezuelan President Nicolas Maduro had burned convoys of Western humanitarian aid when, in fact, the exact opposite was true: the aid trucks had been set on fire by *anti-Maduro* protestors.[19] The point is, again, that lies and outright propaganda are not an anomaly or mistake in the news, but rather are a very part of what the news is.

---

18) "Kefu teito ni tekiki raishū; kyūki o gekitsui, waga songai keibi," *Asahi Shimbun*, 19 April 1942.

19) Glenn Greenwald, "NYT's Exposé on the Lies About Burning Aid Trucks in Venezuela Shows How U.S. Government and Media Spread Pro-War Propoganda," *The Intercept*, March 11, 2019, https://theintercept.com/2019/03/10/nyts-expose-on-the-lies-about-burning-humanitarian-trucks-in-venezuela-shows-how-us-govt-and-media-spread-fake-news/.

6) Reading the news historically

So, how do we get around all these various problems? Should we just give up reading-watching the news altogether? Well, no, that would probably be too extreme. But we do need to change how we consume the news. We need to always read it critically. And I would suggest, especially, that we need to approach it historically. That is to say, we need to read the news like historians do, and especially as historians read historical sources.

When historians use sources, we always approach them critically. We never assume that what is written or reported is the exact truth. Instead, we automatically assume that this is *one perspective* of how a past event occurred. We then try to gather as many perspectives (sources) as possible, to try to reconstruct a more accurate and complete picture of what might have actually happened. But we do not presume that what is written in a single source is the exact or whole truth.

Put simply, there are two main ways to read the news historically. The first is to read the news as you would read a historical source. This means that we should understand that it gives a certain perspective on events. More specifically, we can understand that it shows what or how some people thought, or how the newspaper wanted readers to think, at that time. This is essential if we want to see through propaganda. To cite an example, on August 6th, 1945, US President Harry Truman announced to the world that the first atomic bomb was dropped on Hiroshima. In his speech, which was reported in the news, he said that Hiroshima was "an important Japanese Army base."[20] However, many people then, and almost everyone now, knows that Hiroshima was most certainly *not* just a military base. It was a major urban area with a large, mostly civilian population. But most Americans reading the news at the time would not have known that. Why? Perhaps because if they had known the truth, that the atomic bomb killed hundreds of thousands of innocent civilians, they might have been opposed to them in the first place. So, when historians read such accounts, we understand the distinction between what was reported and the historical truth. We also understand more clearly *why* such untruths might have been reported in the first place: because they had specific goals in mind for shaping how people thought.

---

20) Cited in Ran Zwigenberg, *Hiroshima: The Origins of Global Memory Culture*, (Cambridge: Cambridge University Press, 2014), 26.

The other things that historians do when we read the news as a historical source is to research how news coverage changed over time. This works for almost any topic. You could pick stereotypes about the Japanese in American newspapers, for instance. You could read the news coverage over a long period of time, from the early 20th century to the mid-20th century. At that time, you would see newspapers report on the topic in very different ways. Early 20th century reports might have been filled with negative racial stereotypes. These stereotypes would have intensified during the period of WWII. But following that, after Japan and America became political and economic allies, the coverage would have become much more positive. This is just one example from many. But it works with almost every topic. The important point is that *news coverage changes greatly over time*. So, if you want to know about current events, too, you can't just read current news articles. You must also read old news coverage about the same topic.

The second way to read news historically is to place the topics reported in their own historical contexts. This is important because news coverage almost never explains the detailed history of what it is reporting on. Why did the US fight two wars in Iraq? Why did Russia annex Crimea in 2014 and then start fighting in Ukraine in 2022? If you just listened to current news then or now, you might simply be led to believe that it was because Saddam Hussein or Vladimir Putin were just "bad guys" or were "crazy." But that would not be a very accurate understanding of events at all, and it certainly would not be based on history. Rather, to understand these things, you need to take the news coverage and then research actual historical studies about the events being reported.

How to read the news historically

❖ Distinguish between what actually happened and what was *reported to have happened.*
❖ Ask why events may have been reported in a certain way.
❖ Understand how news coverage changes over time.
❖ Research the historical background and context for current events.

Figure 71: An explanation of how to read the news historically. Composed by Justin Aukema, 2022.

7) Conclusion

In this chapter, we learned what the news is and what are some of its common problems. These included problems relating especially to issues of so-called objectivity and bias. I also proposed an alternative, better way to read and to use the news. This involves going beyond just passively consuming the news and moving toward critically examining it. The way I suggested to do this is to read the news historically. This means understanding the difference between what happened and what was reported, grasping the reasons for why events may have been reported in a certain way, and understanding how news coverage changes over time. Equipped with these tools, you will most certainly be better prepared to read the news. Now, I would like to close with one last example.

When Donald Trump was president of the United States, he liked to call many news outlets "fake news." Many of Donald Trump's opponents, however, did not like this. They said that Trump was just using this as a rhetorical device to dismiss inconvenient truths. But in fact, both sides missed the point. Trump was actually closer to the truth, because he illustrated a point that all historians are already supposed to know: that all news is essentially biased and that much of it contains elements of untruth. However, historians know that even these untruths can be revealing when the reasons and motivations behind them are properly understood. However, Trump's opponents, in arguing that the news was not "fake" but was actually "true" and "authentic," were making an even more dangerous error. They were leading people to believe that there is a difference between fake and real news in the first place. This totally misses the point of what news is, as we have seen in this chapter.

CHAPTER FIFTEEN
Using theory

1) Introduction

This chapter examines how to use theoretical literature and ideas in your essay. But first, what is "theory" 理論 and why do you need it? Well, put simply, as someone once told me, theory is like a sharp knife – it helps you cut through the extraneous material of your topic and see right to the heart of the issue. That is to say, it helps you find the significance of your topic and explain why it is important. So, following that same example, imagine that you are a surgeon (scholar/student) operating on a patient (your topic). Surgery is complicated, and you do not want to go at it alone. You need help. And most importantly, you need *tools*. So, theory is like these tools, or your *toolbox* if you will, to borrow another metaphor. They help you complete your job of writing and conducting research.

Theory or theoretical literature is generally literature or works written, often by philosophers or scholars, on very broad and *abstract* topics. For example, some theoretical literature might deal with ideas of "capital," "space," or "propaganda," as we will see below. All of these are *big* ideas; they are abstract, theoretical ideas. Because theoretical ideas are so big, there is a good chance that some of them will also relate to our research topic, which is usually much smaller. I will give some specific examples on this point shortly. But for the time being, just keep in mind that as you are reading philosophical or theoretical literature, you will want to find elements that connect with your topic and perhaps even help you to reveal

But how and where do we find "theory" in the first place? This is not an easy question to answer. The simple response is that you will need to read *a lot* and *broadly* to first find some theoretical ideas that resonate with you and your topic. These things do not always come immediately. Sometimes, they take a lot of time to discover. My general advice for beginning with theory is first to *familiarize yourself with the classics*. That is to say, have a general idea of the major philosophers, Western cannon or otherwise, and what they thought and said, what they wrote about. You want to have an idea of who these people are and what they wrote about because they come up so frequently in other people's research, and because their ideas influence much about how people think today. So, some general philosophers that come to mind might be Hegel, Kant, Marx, or Nietzsche.

Or you might want to investigate philosophers who are a little more contemporary or modern. These could include Hannah Arendt or Susan Sontag. Or again, maybe you want to familiarize yourself with recent economic history and the history of economic ideas. In this case, you could turn to any number of thinkers from Rosa Luxemburg to John Maynard Keynes, to Paul Sweezy. There are lots of possibilities. It is impossible to discuss or to cover all of them here. In general, though, start with the relatively big names and try to *read some of their actual works* if possible. Of course, it helps to have explanatory texts or secondary texts written on those thinkers as well. But nothing beats to the real thing. If you can read some of their actual texts, even if it is just short segments, do it. Below, I will give some further examples of how to use theory once you have found some ideas that resonate with you.

2) Examples of how to use theory

In this section, I will show you some examples of how to use theory. Most of these come from my previous research experience.

A) *Example 1: Nietzsche and War and Youth*

When I was a master's student in 2011, I researched the literature of Saotome Katsumoto who wrote about the March 10, 1945 Great Tokyo Air Raid. This related to my interest in historical memories of World War II in Japan. Saotome had experienced the Great Tokyo Air Raid as a child and barely survived. Ever since that time, the event remained imprinted in his memory, and he wrote many books that analyzed the bombings and attempted to understand the psychological impacts of the air raids. One of these books, which he wrote in 1991, was called *War and Youth* (*Sensō to seishun*).[21] There was also a film adaption of this book released that same year. I analyzed this book and film and discussed its significance, as well as the important meanings of much of the symbolism in the film.

One important symbol in the film was a telephone pole that had been burned in the 1945 air raid. The pole was a potent reminder of the terror of the raid for survivors and it served as an opportunity for younger generations to learn more about the Great Tokyo Air Raid, too. This was the case for the story's main protagonist, Yukari, whose father and aunt experienced the air raid and had traumatic memories of the event ever since. Yukari listens to the war stories of her father and aunt, and eventually decides to help preserve the telephone pole and prevent it from being torn down. In my analysis, I determined that this event was highly significant and symbolic. It seemed clear to me that the characters were trying to preserve the past in order to help teach future generations about the terrors of war and the importance of peace. Moreover, this seemed very similar to the writings of Friedrich Nietzsche on the preservation of history that I had also read around the same time.[22] So, I was able to connect this theoretical literature with my own topic, and to combine them into an analysis as follows.

25

reasons for the causes of the Pacific War aided by a willful forgetfulness – he writes, acts as a

hindrance to meaningful action and, with words that echo Nietzsche's thoughts on the

monumental view of history, is "...the great memory-desiring machine to recall the violence of

the past in order to act in the present, even though the act of memorization is often made to serve

as a substitute for acting."[45] Unlike Nietzsche, however, Harotoonian does not reflect on other

possible views of history, for example, the critical view, of which Nietzsche explains, acts "in the

service of life." He identifies this further writing,

> Man must have the strength to break up the past; and to apply it too, in order to live. He
> must bring the past to the bar of judgment, interrogate it remorselessly, and finally
> condemn it. Every past is worth condemning: this is the rule in mortal affairs, which
> always contain a large measure of human power and human weakness.[46]

---

21) Saotome Katsumoto, *Sensō to seishun*, (Tokyo: Kōdansha, 1991).
22) The essay I am thinking of is "On the Uses and Disadvantages of History for Life." See Friedrich Nietzsche, *Untimely Meditations*, Translated by R.J. Hollingdale, Edited by Daniel Breazeale, (Cambridge: Cambridge University Press, 1999).

Literature and film of atrocity offer, by their very nature, critical views of history. Unlike the Tsukuru-kai and other revisionist groups, which work to alter the past and present it at a glorious fetish, to make of it a monument, literature, like that of Saotome Katsumoto on the air raids, and films such as *The Human Condition, Black Rain*, and *War and Youth* are critical of the past. One does not leave these films with the impression that war is a glorious thing, or that one side or individual fought with noble and honorable sacrifice. Rather, because they are explicit in placing the guilt on all sides involved, and on showing that war only begets suffering, one leaves with a renewed understanding of the senselessness of war and violence.

Moreover, *War and Youth* aligns with Nietzsche's view that "the knowledge of the past is only desired for the service of the future and the present, not to weaken the present or undermine a living future."[47] In other words, the film does not hope to stagnate or wallow in the past, as some scholars like Harotoonian have suggested is a trend in Japanese scholarship, but rather uses

---

[45] Yoda, Tomiko and Harry Harootunian eds. *Japan After Japan: Social and Cultural Life from the Recessionary 1990s to the Present.* (Durham: Duke University Press, 2006), 98.
[46] Nietzsche, 106.
[47] Nietzsche, 106.

26

the past in order to act in the present. This is reflected both in the creation of the film and throughout the story. During the creation of the film, both Saotome and Tadashi expressed their hope that the film would help convey the horrors of war to a society that was presently launching a terrible and destructive war in Iraq. Through an example of the past, the film's creators hoped to positively influence the present.

In the final scenes of the film, after Yukari manages to both write her report (confront the past) and make others aware of the importance of the telephone pole as a living reminder, we see her portrayed with a renewed sense of vigor and enthusiasm for life. She plays with fireworks with the neighborhood children and skips off to school with her brother. The audience understands, however, that this is not a happiness that comes from ignorance, but the happiness that comes from a renewed sense of appreciation for life. It is this sense that is the biggest benefit of confronting and learning from the past – a sense that will help one act in the present, a sense that will help one live, and appreciate life.

Figure 72: Unpublished research paper by Justin Aukema, 2011.

As the above example shows, I used Nietzsche's "On the Use and Abuse of History," a famous short book, to elaborate more about my topic. I was initially attracted to this book because I was studying history and I wanted to know what Nietzsche wrote about history. I found his ideas highly enlightening at the time, and so I used them in my analysis for my research. Specifically, I pointed to his idea of "monumental" versus "critical" history, to show that the preservation of the past, in this case the telephone pole, can have important critical implications for the present, in this case teaching future generations about peace and the Tokyo Air Raids.

B) *Example two: propaganda in film*

Now, let's look at one more example. In 2011, I wrote a seminar course paper on WWII propaganda films, particularly cartoons and animation films, in Japan and the US. Note that I previously discussed this topic in an earlier chapter in this textbook. The object of that paper was simple: I wanted to understand how WWII US propaganda cartoons produced by Disney and working with the Office of War Information portrayed the Japanese. I was already aware that such films relied heavily on racist stereotypes and misinformation designed to get the American populace to hate, fear, and despise the enemy "Other." But I also needed some more background information.

Namely, I needed to know and define precisely what "propaganda" was, in the first place. Propaganda is a word that is often thrown around. But what is the definition? What kinds of propaganda are there? These are questions that I needed to answer when setting out to analyze my research topic. So, I picked up two books to help me with this. One was, simply, the *Encyclopedia Britannica*, which I accessed online. Here, I looked up the dictionary definition of "propaganda." Yet this did not give me a full picture, particularly of the various ways in which propaganda had been used and utilized throughout history. To understand more about this, I needed to know the *history of the concept*. And this connection to the *conceptual*, meant that I needed to turn to more *theoretical* literature. Toward this end, I used a book by Stanley Cunningham called *The Idea of Propaganda: A Reconstruction* (2002).[23] With these two sources, I could develop a theoretical, conceptual, and historical framework for discussing what propaganda was. And then I could use this framework to help me analyze my

---

23) Stanley Cunningham, *The Idea of Propaganda: A Reconstruction*, (Westport: Praeger Publishers, 2002).

own topic of WWII historical films. Thus, I added my discussion of propaganda to the very front of my research paper, right after the introduction. It looked like this:

5

Hollywood and the U.S. Government

The negative associations that the word *propaganda* has come to acquire are vast, and deeply imbedded in public consciousness, drawing to mind some kind of attack or assault is being made on our higher functioning facilities to think, and willing us to act, think or feel a certain way, whether in line with our own volitional will or against. Additionally, *propaganda* could just as easily draw to mind images of government control and oversight, all of which gain increasing importance during such times of distress as war.

While the concept of *propaganda* has changed over time, as has the way in people view it, it is possible to narrow down some of the elements which characterize the term. Some of these, for example, would be that propaganda is "dissemination of information – facts, arguments, rumors, half-truths, or lies – to influence public opinion." While propagandists do not always use outright lies, they will often "emphasize the elements of information that support their position and deemphasize or exclude those that do not."[3] With such one sided views of things, propaganda poses as real communication but is in fact defective information. Further, it disregards higher values such as truth or truthfulness, and promotes an acceptance of unquestioned, unexamined beliefs. To make their message seem less threatening and more neutral propagandists often use words like "information."[4]

Propaganda and its producers are not some far away construct, practiced only in authoritarian regimes and by malicious governments. Quite to the contrary, different forms of propaganda bombard everyone to the extent that the average mind becomes overwhelmed on a

---

[3] *Encyclopedia Britannica Online.* Encyclopedia Britannica, 2011. Web. 26 Jan. 2011.
http://www.britannica.com/EBchecked/topic/478875/propaganda
[4] Cunningham, Stanley B. *The Idea of Propaganda: A Reconstruction.* (Westport, CT: Praeger Publishers, 2002), 176-178.

6

quite regular basis. Moreover, as the Encyclopedia Britannica entry on propaganda states, "nearly every significant government, political party, special-interest group, social movement, and big business firm in the advanced countries," makes use of propaganda to sway public opinion, influence consumer purchasing habits, and propagate a certain position.[5]

Images have especially strong power when used for propagandistic purposes. Images create something which resembles reality, and upon being viewed, becomes the audiences' new reality. For the viewer, the image hangs suspended between imagination and sense and acts as a mediator or a lens through which the viewer then makes further judgments about reality. The staying power of the image is also important and its other function as a symbol assures that it is easily recollected by the viewer, and draws on deeply held emotions and beliefs.[6]

Before the World War II, the American government was well aware of the connotations that words like "propaganda" and "censorship" brought up and, because of the excesses of wartime propaganda in World War I, was not anxious to give any kind of impression that they were engaging in propagating the public. It was in this light that, at the beginning of the War, President Roosevelt would issue statements about wanting "no censorship of the motion picture."[7] Nevertheless, under the guise of buzz words like "information" and "education," government agencies were eventually created to put forth the government's position on issues relating the war, and mobilize the public behind the war effort. One such agency was the Office of War Information, which was charged with the responsibility of utilizing the motion picture industry and getting Hollywood to do its part in fighting the war.

---

[5] Ibid.
[6] Cunningham, 128-169.
[7] Doherty, Thomas. *Projections of War: Hollywood, American Culture, and World War II.* (New York: Columbia University Press, 1993), 45.

Figure 73: Unpublished research paper by Justin Aukema, 2011.

So, as you can see from the above example, I use some theoretical and practical literature to discuss what "propaganda" is and how it has been used. I note, for example, that propaganda is "defective information" which is used in all kinds of situations, not just wartime, to influence behavior. I then connect this discussion to my research topic of WWII propaganda films.

This example illustrates that theory doesn't necessarily need to be overly complicated or even philosophical. It could simply be a conceptual history, the history of an *idea*, such as propaganda, which you can then connect to your research.

C) *Example three: Marx, Lefebvre, and Space*

The third and final example I want to give of how to use theory comes from my 2020 Ph.D. dissertation, "Senseki: Memories, Narratives, and Ideologies at Japanese War Sites."[24] In this dissertation, I used lots of theoretical theory and literature. Much more, in fact, than I had previously used in my other research papers. The topic of my dissertation was Japanese war sites, or *sensō iseki* in Japanese. I wanted to understand how these sites, which included old war-damaged or military buildings and facilities, had been used throughout history, how they had come to be preserved in some cases, and how they were being used in the present. This connects to my previous interest in the historical memory of WWII and issues of historical preservation. For instance, in Example one in this chapter, I discussed Saotome Katsumoto's air raid literature and the preservation of an old, air-raid-burned telephone pole. So, my dissertation topic on war sites was similar to, and in many ways was a continuation of, such earlier topics.

In my dissertation, one thing that I wanted to know was *who* had built various war sites and *why*. I thought that this would have an important impact on how those sites were later either remembered or forgotten. But the reasons behind this were not always clear to me. So, I decided to turn to theoretical literature, in this case on the concept of *space* 空間. Basically, this is because I realized that war sites were not just *objects* per se but were rather *spaces* where people would later come and in some cases reflect on the war and recall past memories. They were also spaces that were being used to teach future generations about war.

As I researched about "space," I came across the ideas of French theorist,

---

24) Justin Aukema, "Senseki: Memories, Narratives, and Ideologies at Japanese War Sites," Unpublished Ph.D. Dissertation. Presented at Sophia University, 2020.

Henri Lefebvre, and specifically his book titled *The Production of Space* (1974).[25] Lefebvre's ideas are too complicated to accurately summarize here. But, put simply, he drew from Karl Marx to argue that space is A) socially produced and that, therefore, it B) reflects the dominant ideas, aesthetics, and ideologies of the ruling class (at that particular time). Furthermore, in order to understand how Lefebvre arrived at this conclusion, I in fact needed to dig further into theoretical literature. In this case, I needed to understand some of Marx's writings, since these were influential for Lefebvre. So, in this regard, for example, Marx wrote in *The German Ideology* (1846) that:

The ideas of the ruling class are in every epoch the ruling ideas: i.e., the class which is the ruling material force of society, is at the same time its ruling intellectual force. The class which has the means of material production at its disposal, has control at the same time over the means of mental production, so that thereby, generally speaking, the ideas of those who lack the means of mental production are subject to it.[26]

In fact, this is a key Marxist concept, and it is quite well known. "The ideas of the ruling class are in every epoch the ruling ideas." So, this means that what people think, feel, and believe are influenced, first, by their proximity to the means of reproduction, i.e., their class, and that, second, the main or dominant ideas will be those of the ruling, in this case capitalist, class.

What did this mean for Lefebvre? Well, it is easy to see some overlap, even just by comparing his main argument. So, Lefebvre said, for example, that: *"(Social) space is a (social) product,"* and thus he continued to say that:

Schematicaly speaking, each society offers up its own peculiar space, as it were, as an 'object' for analysis and overall theoretical explication. I say each society, but it would be more accurate to say each mode of production, along with its specific relations of production.[27]

We can see how this is similar, because, like Marx, Lefebvre says that space is socially determined and that its meanings etc. are determined by the dominant

---

25) Henri Lefebvre, *The Production of Space*, Translated by Donald Nicholson-Smith, (Malden: Wiley-Blackwell, 1992).

26) From *The German Ideology*. In Karl Marx and Friedrich Engels, *The Marx-Engels Reader*. Edited by Robert C. Tucker. 2nd Revised & Enlarged edition. (New York: W. W. Norton & Company, 1978).

27) Lefebvre, *The Production of Space*, pp. 26, 31.

modes and relations of production. That is to say, they reflect class desires and concerns. This thus draws directly from Marx's statement in *The German Ideology.*

Knowing this, therefore, I decided in my dissertation that Japanese war sites, too, were forms of socially produced space, and that, accordingly, they reflected dominant class concerns and ideologies. Namely, at the time they were produced, they reflected the concerns and desires of the ruling class and the military. But later, in the postwar, they obtained other meanings and uses that reflected other class relations. Lefebvre also argued that the meanings and uses of space were not fixed per se but that they could also be used to challenge dominant ideology. This was like the use of "counter-monuments" or "counter-memory," or even the notion that challenges to capitalism emerge from within capitalism itself. So, I used this, too, to suggest that war sites could be used to challenge dominant ideologies of war and militarism, and instead send messages of peace. Sections of my dissertation on this subject looked as follows:

Theories of space and spatially situated memories

The notion of "socially produced space" originated with the French theorist Henri Lefebvre, who posited that each society and epoch create their own social space that reflects the dominant ethos, social relations, and modes of production of the day. Since Lefebvre's main concern was the aleatory effects of fetishized capitalist space and not war memory, this dissertation makes no systematic attempt to apply his thought to the study of Japanese war sites. Nevertheless, his findings are relevant in that they highlight A) that the meanings of space are socially determined and subject to change; B) that space is intertwined with larger ideologies and hierarchies of power; and C) that space emerges through complex and overlapping relationships between objects, representations, and lived social practices.[2] This approach enables this dissertation to adopt the aforementioned triadic view of Japanese war sites as a network of acts, objects, and discourses each concerned with the meanings and memories of the wartime past.

Figure 74: A section of the author's unpublished 2020 Ph.D. dissertation. © Justin Aukema, 2020.

3) Conclusion

This chapter offered a brief glimpse at how to use theory in our academic research writing. Using theory is not easy. In fact, that is why I saved it for the very last chapter of this textbook! But it *is* a highly important step in the research project and one which will be essential for us as we move forward, especially writing our graduation capstone paper eventually. To summarize, the key points are as follows. First, read broadly among the theoretical literature. Second, start with the classics, the big names, and the big thinkers. Do not delve into marginal stuff right away. Of course, this is important, too, and you can make great discoveries here. But you need to have some understanding of the basic theoretical frameworks for discussion. And names like Plato and Kant will be indispensable here. Third, find something that resonates with and speaks to your research topic. Theory can be difficult, and we may not even understand fully much of what we read. In fact, scholars today still argue over how to interpret philosophical texts. Perhaps much of their value lies in the fact that they can be interpreted in various ways. But, in any case, read until you find something that you do understand, and which speaks to you. Use this, think about it deeply, and consider how it relates to your topic. Particularly, you want to use theory to illuminate something *new*, some new insight about your topic that might not otherwise be apparent. This is the real value of using theory. You also may simply want to use it to give yourself a framework for analysis. This was the case in my discussion of "propaganda." Sometimes it is necessary just to analyze and to understand the history of an idea and how such ideas have changed over time. This is an easier way to use theory, but one which can be equally important and insightful.

APPENDICES

"Argumentative-opinion essay"	**"Problem-solution essay"**	**"Agree-disagree (IELTS)"**

"Argumentative-opinion essay"

INTRODUCTION
Hook (Catch your reader's attention)
Connecting sentences
Thesis

REASON 1
Topic sentence
Supporting sentence(s)
Evidence
(Concluding or transition sentence)

REASON 2
Topic sentence
Supporting sentence(s)
Evidence
(Concluding or transition sentence)

CONCLUSION
Restate thesis
Suggestion/opinion/prediction

"Problem-solution essay"

INTRODUCTION
Paraphrase question
Outline sentence

PROBLEM
Explain the problem in more detail
Discuss some of the causes of the problem
Discuss some of the negative effects/results
of this problem
(Details and examples)

SOLUTION
Propose your solution to the problem
Explain how this will help solve the problem
Details and examples

CONCLUSION
Summary of the main points
Prediction or recommendation

"Agree-disagree (IELTS)"

INTRODUCTION
Restate problem
State your opinion (agree/disagree)

REASONS
Reason 1 + Support
Reason 2 + Support
(Concluding sentence)

COUNTER/RESTATE ARGUMENT
Explain one of the most common counter
arguments
Restate your argument + Support (i.e.
your argument is better)

CONCLUSION
Restate your opinion
Recommendation

Appendix 1: Three different types of essay writing

Appendix 2: Example of a completed argumentative essay (literature theme)

Justin Aukema
Freshman Seminar Course
Spring 2022

Memories of Sin as a Karmic Cycle in
Natsume Sōseki's "The Third Night"

Intro

Natsume Sōseki is one of Japan's most famous writers. He is known for writing realistic human dramas and novels such as *Bochan* (*Bochan*, 1906) and *And Then* (*Sore kara*, 1909). Sōseki also wrote magical realist fiction and even science fiction stories. One of the most famous of these works is *Ten Nights of Dreams* (*Yume jūya*, 1908). In this short essay, I focus on one section of *Ten Nights of Dreams*, "The Third Night," and I argue that the chapter is a metaphor for sin, guilt, and rebirth that borrows heavily from Buddhist imagery and symbolism.

thesis statement 主張

story summary

"The Third Night" is narrated from the perspective of an unnamed protagonist, presumably a middle-aged man, who, for reasons initially unbeknownst to him, is carrying a young, blind child on his back through a dark forest. At various points in the story, the relationship between the two is described as that between parent and child; however, there are also further indications that this portrayal is rather simply for allegorical purposes. The story progresses with the "child" directing his "father" along a path toward an unspecified location only known to the child. From the beginning, it is made clear through various examples of foreshadowing that some unspeakable past event of great significance has transpired between the two characters, and yet which simultaneously is hidden from the main character's memory. The following conversation, for instance, indicates this lopsided historical remembrance:

> "It was just such an evening," said the voice as though to itself.
> "What was?" I asked in tones that betrayed the feeling that something had only just failed to strike home.
> "What was? But you know well enough," the child answered scornfully. And then I began to feel that I had some idea of what it was all about (29).

Quotations longer than five lines should be written like this and indented one full cm on each side *elaborate main argument*

The progression of the story and the characters along the path also mirrors the movement toward the revelation of the truth of this event, which is simultaneously revealed to both the protagonist and the reader by the child only at the very end of the story. Upon arriving at a cedar tree in the forest, the child discloses that the protagonist murdered a blind man at this spot exactly one-hundred years ago. Subsequently, the child is described as becoming "as heavy as a god of stone" (30), and the story abruptly ends.

The Buddhist imagery abundantly sprinkled throughout the story indicates that this brief

supporting evidence and examples

vignette is in fact a broader analogy for a hellish afterlife, and a metaphor for sin, guilt, and rebirth. For instance, the story begins by describing the age of the child as six years old. This is likely no coincidence, since there are likewise six cycles of rebirth, Saṃsāra in English or the rokudō in Japanese, awaiting humans in the Buddhist afterlife. And the first of these, the lowest rung promised to all sinners and those bearing the guilt of heavy crimes is indeed hell (jigoku-dō). Thus, from the outset of the story, the reader is given indication of where this story truly takes place: not in an earthly forest, but rather on a hellish metaphysical plane. This explains the seemingly inexplicable fact that the event of the murder described by the child

cite text page numbers

happened one hundred years ago (30). There are also many other indications that the scene *example* described is hell, especially regarding the child who is described as an gohōzu in the Japanese text – a demon-like monster – and an "incubus" in the English version (29).

It is also clear that the child represents the weight of the protagonist's crime of murder and his feelings of guilt over this. Consider the following conversation found at the initial *example* stages of their journey:

> "Father, am I heavy?"
> "No, not heavy."
> "Wait. I'll be heavy soon" (28)

evidence/example

This is coupled with the scene at the end when, after the protagonist is reminded of the true nature of his crime, the child suddenly becomes "as heavy as a god of stone" (30). Thus, the

2

metaphorical weight of the child in fact represents the weight of the knowledge of truth and sin

regarding the man's crimes, as well as his feelings of guilt that this realization brings. And, in

keeping with the Buddhist imagery, it is no coincidence, therefore, that "god of stone" in the

Japanese original is in fact "Jizo," a common Buddhist statue.

example   The abrupt end of the story, the main character's progression through forgetting and

remembrance, and the final appearance of the Jizo statue, furthermore, indicates that the

protagonist may be doomed to repeat this scene. The notion of Saṃsāra is based on the idea of

atoning for past *karma* (Jp. *katsuma*) – whether good or bad – and misdeeds in the hope of

moving on to the next level of rebirth and eventually reaching the final stage of Deva (Jp.

tendō) amongst the heavenly beings. Yet Jizo also indicates atonement for unfulfilled karma

and is commonly associated with an afterlife consisting of the near-endless piling of heavy

stones in order to make up for past pain and suffering caused. In the case of "The Third Night,"

it seems that the protagonist's first task is simply one of remembering and confronting the

painful and suppressed truth about the nature of his own sinful actions. Moreover, the fact that

the main character doesn't arrive at the truth of his own accord, but rather has it revealed *to*

him only at the very end, indicates that his progression through the cycle of rebirth is still going

to be a long road.

Conclusion   "The Third Night," like the rest of the stories in *Ten Nights of Dreams*, are all fictional

figments of another narrator's imagination. This, however, makes the importance of deducing

symbolism and metaphor in these short vignettes all the more pressing. In "The Third Night," *restate main argument*

Sōseki relied heavily on Buddhist imagery to convey a state of willful forgetting in response

to one's own shameful acts. Yet the overall message is a harsh reminder that the first task of

atonement is frequently to confront painful truths.

Works cited   bibliography

Goosen, Theodore (ed.). *The Oxford Book of Japanese Short Stories*. Oxford University Press, 2010.

Sōseki, Natsume. "Yume jūya." *Natsume Sōseki Zenshū*, Vol. 10. Chikuma bunko, 1996.

BIBLIOGRAPHY

"Agaranai chingin 'Nihon dake ga ijō,' motomerareru seisaku no kenshō." *Tōkyō Shimbun.* June 15, 2022. https://www.tokyo-np.co.jp/article/183402.

Andō, Hiroshige III. *Shimbashi Station.* 1874. Accessed at MIT Visualizing Cultures. https://visualizingcultures.mit.edu/throwing_off_asia_01/gallery/pages/Y0185_TOA.htm.

Aukema, Justin. "At the Border of Memory and History: Kyoto's Contested War Heritage." In Edward Boyle (ed). *Heritage, Conflicted Sites and Bordered Memories in Asia.* Brill (forthcoming 2022).

Aukema, Justin. "Modernization Theory & Japanese Veterans' Asia-Pacific 'War Tales.'" *The Asia-Pacific Journal: Japan Focus,* Vol. 20, Iss. 10, No. 5 (May 2022).

Aukema, Justin. "Senseki: Memories, Narratives, and Ideologies at Japanese War Sites." Unpublished Ph.D. Dissertation. Presented at Sophia University, 2020.

"Bei, ei gekimetsu kokumin taikai." *Kyōto hinode shinbun.* December 11, 1941.

Cunningham, Stanley. *The Idea of Propaganda: A Reconstruction.* Westport: Praeger Publishers, 2002.

Daijūroku Shidan Shireibu (ed.). *Manshū haken kinen shashin-chō.* Kyoto: Daijūroku Shidan Shireibu, 1936. Kyoto Institute, Library and Archives, Serial Number KO 396.9 D19, Material ID 110296549.

Gluck, Carol. *Japan's Modern Myths: Ideology in the Late Meiji Period.* Princeton University Press, 1985.

Greenwald, Glenn. "NYT's Exposé on the Lies About Burning Aid Trucks in Venezuela Shows How U.S. Government and Media Spread Pro-War Propaganda." *The Intercept.* March 11, 2019. https://theintercept.com/2019/03/10/nyts-expose-on-the-lies-about-burning-humanitarian-trucks-in-venezuela-shows-how-us-govt-and-media-spread-fake-news/.

Hallman, Carly. "Who Owns Your News? The Top 100 Digital News Outlets and Their

164

Ownership." *Titlemax*. https://www.titlemax.com/discovery-center/lifestyle/who-owns-your-news-the-top-100-digital-news-outlets-and-their-ownership/.

"Ianfu" o sakujo, dai 32 gun shireibu-gō no setsumei-ban, ken ga hōshin kettei." *Ryūkyū Shinpo*. February 24, 2012.

International Monetary Fund. "SDR Valuation." https://www.imf.org/external/np/fin/data/rms_sdrv.aspx.

International Monetary Fund. "Total IMF Credit Outstanding." August 22, 2022. https://www.imf.org/external/np/fin/tad/balmov2.aspx?type=TOTAL.

"Jūman no teki Masani senmetsu." *Kyōto hinode shinbun*. December 14, 1937.

"Jūroku shidan shireibu kinō Manshū e." *Kyōto Hinode Shinbun*. April 6, 1929.

"Kefu teito ni tekiki raishū; kyūki o gekitsui, waga songai keibi." *Asahi Shimbun*. April 19, 1942.

Kutsuma Yasuji, Kyoto Shimbun-sha (eds.). *Sakimori no shi*. Kyoto: Kyoto Shimbun, 1976-1994.

Kyoto-shi Rekishi Shiryō-kan. "Kyoto no hakuran-kai." 2008. https://www2.city.kyoto.lg.jp/somu/rekishi/fm/nenpyou/htmlsheet/toshi29.html.

Lefebvre, Henri. *The Production of Space*. Translated by Donald Nicholson-Smith. 1 edition. Malden: Wiley-Blackwell, 1992.

Lubetsky, Michael, Charles LeBeau, and David Harrington. *Discover Debate: Basic Skills for Supporting and Refuting Opinions*. Language Solutions Incorporated (2000).

Marx, Karl and Friedrich Engels. *The Marx-Engels Reader*. Edited by Robert C. Tucker. 2nd Revised & Enlarged edition. New York: W. W. Norton & Company, 1978.

McClain, James L. *Japan: A Modern History*. W.W. Norton & Company, 2002.

Mizuno, Toshikata. *Captain Higuchi (Higuchi Taii)*. Meiji Era woodblock print. April 1895. Photograph copyright 2022 Museum of Fine Arts, Boston. Jean S. and Frederic A. Sharf Collection, 2000.439a-c.

Naimushō Jinja-kyoku. "Gokoku jinja seido no kakuritsu." *Shūhō*, No. 131 (April 1939): 2-8.

Nakamura, Shūkō. *Great Naval Victory off Haiyang Island (Kaiyōtō oki nikkan dai-shōri)*. Meiji Era woodblock print. October 1984. Photograph copyright 2022 Museum of Fine Arts, Boston. Jean S. and Frederic A. Sharf Collection 2000.380.11a-c.

Okinawa Prefectural Assembly. General Meeting No. 4. Kayo Sogi. February 24, 2012.

Okinawa Prefectural Assembly. General Meeting No. 4. Shimoji Hiroshi. February 24, 2012.

"Pontocho kaburenjō 2." Kyoto Institute, Library and Archives digital archives. Serial No: Shashin 012, Photo No. 466.

Rohter, Larry. "New Doubts Raised Over Famous War Photo." *The New York Times*. August 17, 2009. https://www.nytimes.com/2009/08/18/arts/design/18capa.html.

Satterfield, Susan. "Livy and the Pax Deum." *Classical Philology* 111, Number 2 (April 2016): 165-176.

Shirakawa, Tetsuo. *"Senbotsusha irei" to kindai Nihon: Jun'nansha to gokoku jinja no seiritsu-shi*. Bensei shuppan. 2015.

"Teki no iki shitai hachi, kyūman." *Kyōto hinode shinbun*. December 19, 1937.

Yokohama City. "Shishikō, shishi, shishiII." October 28, 2020. https://www.city.yokohama.lg.jp/kurashi/kyodo-manabi/library/shiru/history/shishi.html

Mitsui bunko. *Shiryō ga kataru Mitsui no ayumi: Echigoya kara Mitsui zaibatsu*. Tokyo: Yoshikawa Kōbunkan, 2015.

"Nankin e Nankin e." *Kyōto Hinode Shinbun*. December 2, 1937.

"Nankin otsu! Kyōraku no kofun." *Kyōto hinode shinbun*. December 10, 1937.

"Nekkyō shimin no geiha e, gaisen ressha tōchaku su." *Kyōto Hinode Shinbun*. June 7, 1936.

Nietzsche, Friedrich. *Untimely Meditations*. Translated by R.J. Hollingdale. Edited by Daniel Breazeale. Cambridge: Cambridge University Press, 1999.

"Ōno konchū butai nakayama mon ichiban nori." *Kyōto Hinode Shinbun*. December 14, 1937.

Saaler, Sven. "The Problems of Science Management: Riken Is No Isolated Case." *Nippon.com*. April 16, 2014. https://www.nippon.com/en/column/g00162/.

Saotome, Katsumoto. *Sensō to seishun*. Tokyo: Kōdansha, 1991.

"Sōkyū ni katsu katsu gunkutsu natsukashi." *Kyōto Hinode Shinbun*. June 6, 1936.

"Tanku gōgō to to ōji o kōshin." *Kyōto Hinode Shinbun*. March 21, 1934.

SCAP/GHQ. "Shinto Directive." December 15, 1945. National Diet Library. Call No. SCA-1 R2, ID 000006847549.

Zwigenberg, Ran. *Hiroshima: The Origins of Global Memory Culture*. Cambridge: Cambridge University Press, 2014.

INDEX

OMUP

大阪公立大学出版会（OMUP）とは
本出版会は、大阪の5公立大学－大阪市立大学、大阪府立大学、大阪女子大学、大阪
府立看護大学、大阪府立看護大学医療技術短期大学部－の教授を中心に2001年に設立
された大阪公立大学共同出版会を母体としています。2005年に大阪府立の4大学が統
合されたことにより、公立大学は大阪府立大学と大阪市立大学のみになり、2022年に
その両大学が統合され、大阪公立大学となりました。これを機に、本出版会は大阪公
立大学出版会（Osaka Metropolitan University Press「略称：OMUP」）と名称を改め、
現在に至っています。なお、本出版会は、2006年から特定非営利活動法人（NPO）と
して活動しています。

About Osaka Metropolitan University Press (OMUP)
Osaka Metropolitan University Press was originally named Osaka Municipal
Universities Press and was founded in 2001 by professors from Osaka City
University, Osaka Prefecture University, Osaka Women's University, Osaka
Prefectural College of Nursing, and Osaka Prefectural Medical Technology College.
Four of these universities later merged in 2005, and a further merger with Osaka
City University in 2022 resulted in the newly-established Osaka Metropolitan
University. On this occasion, Osaka Municipal Universities Press was renamed to
Osaka Metropolitan University Press (OMUP). OMUP has been recognized as a
Non-Profit Organization (NPO) since 2006.

Essential Academic Skills for University Research:
A Historical Studies Perspective

2023年3月20日　発行

著　者　Justin Aukema
発行者　八木　孝司
発行所　大阪公立大学出版会（ＯＭＵＰ）
　　　　〒599-8531　大阪府堺市中区学園町1－1
　　　　大阪公立大学内
　　　　TEL　072（251）6533
　　　　FAX　072（254）9539
印刷所　石川特殊特急製本株式会社